T0321154

doping

doping

a sporting history

April Henning and **Paul Dimeo**

Reaktion Books

Published by
REAKTION BOOKS LTD
Unit 32, Waterside
44–48 Wharf Road
London N1 7UX, UK

www.reaktionbooks.co.uk

First published 2022

Printed and bound in Great Britain
by TJ Books Ltd, Padstow, Cornwall

A catalogue record for this book is available from the British Library

ISBN 978 1 78914 527 4

Contents

Introduction

Sport is unique; there is no other industry like it. Popular competitions like the Olympics or football World Cup attract audiences in the billions. The most successful athletes are household names. There is an economy in and around sport that creates wealth for athletes, managers, coaches, owners, sponsors, media companies and gaming companies, and perhaps less obviously also for doctors, lawyers, bureaucrats, psychologists and writers.

While performance and spectacle are the entertainment end of the business, sport has a long association with health, community, leisure and recreation for participants of all ages. Regular physical activity is considered essential for children's development – physically, mentally and academically. It is also linked to better health for young and older adults. Sport is not the only form of physical activity, but local clubs can provide opportunities for regular exercise, competition and sociability. Schools provide formal physical education and informal daily exercise; sport in school is considered so important that many governments legislate to ensure it happens and fund the training of specialist teachers.

The role of drugs in these contexts is more complex than simple assertions of drug-free or clean sport would have us believe. We have come to expect the 'good' of anti-doping and clean sport, and the criticism of dopers as corrupt cheats trying to short-cut their way to victory. Yet for much of the twentieth century, there was simply no concept of doping, let alone the opinion that it constituted cheating, and consequently there was no prohibition of it. Accounts are rare, but we know that strychnine was given to the top marathon runners in the Olympics in 1904 and 1908, and in 1925 the manager of Arsenal Football Club wrote a detailed description of giving pep pills to all his players for Cup ties against rivals West Ham United.

The first stirrings of regulation were sporadic. A rule forbidding drug use was written for the 1908 Olympic marathon but there is no sign of any other rules until a 1928 statement by the International Amateur Athletic Federation (IAAF) banned artificial stimulants. This was replicated in 1938 by the International Olympic Committee (IOC). However, there was no structured set of rules that could be supported by testing until the mid-1960s.

The groundwork for these rules was started by a group of Italian scientists based in Florence who focused their attention on the use of amphetamines by cyclists and football players. The death of Danish cyclist Knud Enemark Jensen during the 1960 Olympics proved a catalyst to IOC efforts, even though its attribution to doping turned out to be false. Anti-doping gradually emerged as a policy through international meetings in Europe and the determination of the IOC to organize testing during their quadrennial Games. While some leading cyclists openly admitted using stimulants, the feeling among some powerful sports leaders was that sport should be 'clean'.

Quite what that meant and how to achieve it would foment the controversies of the late twentieth and early twenty-first centuries. The explosion of steroid use in the 1970s meant that testing in competition only was practically useless in terms of prevention. These drugs were used for training and muscle-building. Even when a test for them was discovered in 1975, getting access to athletes outside of competitions would be the major challenge.

The scandals of the 1980s were only the tip of the iceberg. Some countries had organized steroid programmes that ran for decades without their leading athletes being caught. By the 1990s, many athletes – with the support of their team doctors and coaches – were using a complex pharmacology of different drugs, masking agents and blood-manipulation processes. Sports authorities were powerless: disorganized, under-resourced, always one step behind the users. They could only complain about the lack of support for anti-doping, criticize dopers and promote fear-mongering messages about the supposed fatal risks of doping. Journalists latched on to scandals with hyperbolic narratives of athletes so determined to win that they would dope themselves into an early grave in exchange for sporting success.

By the 1990s, news from the former East Germany, cycling scandals and suspicions of systemic doping all underpinned the formation of the World Anti-Doping Agency (WADA). This organization would be closely linked to the IOC, which would provide 50 per cent of its funding. The organization's presidency would rotate between an IOC member and a non-IOC member and its committee structure would be based on IOC governance systems. The notion of Olympism was central to the rationale for anti-doping set out in the first World Anti-Doping Code (WADC) in 2003. The rules focused on individual events – there is hardly any mention of team sports. The punishments for countries' non-compliance included not being allowed to host the Olympics. The inevitable conflict of interest came to the fore in the mid-2010s when WADA wanted Russia banned from the 2016 Summer Olympics in Rio de Janeiro, but the IOC allowed many Russian athletes to compete under a neutral flag.

Athletes were hardly consulted in the development of a highly structured anti-doping policy. WADA introduced systems of surveillance and penalties that would not be acceptable in any other walk of life, based on a monopoly of power with no requirement for engagement with those the policy affected. It was athletes who were worse off under the WADC. They could be tested anywhere and at any time. They were responsible for understanding what was acceptable and what was not. They were responsible for any substance found in their sample, regardless of how it got there. No organization was obliged to educate them on these matters. Their privacy and dignity were ignored in the rules, which required drug control officers (DCOs) to observe the urine leaving their body for the sample. They faced bans: initially for two years, raised to four years in the 2009 version of the Code. If they wanted to appeal, the process was expensive, prolonged and destabilizing for their reputation and career, and they were very unlikely to win, as they could not appeal to a civil court, only to the Court of Arbitration for Sport (CAS). They lost legal rights to protect their career and income, and (if their sport had signed up to the WADC) any right to form a trade union to discuss the rules. The stigma of being labelled a doper would last a lifetime, undermining chances for employment in and out of sport. Yet it was easy to fall foul of this system by accident, and though mistakes in the scientific analyses happened they were hard for any wronged athlete to prove.

WADA was supported by the simple message sold to the public that its business was to protect athletes' health and the fairness and integrity of sport. Yet athletes were treated with suspicion – not just those who were caught, or even those at high risk of doping, but all athletes. They were told how to behave. They were not given a voice. Trust was eroded by an excess of monitoring, designed to prop up the public and commercial image of sport as a social good. Meanwhile, sports organizations accepted the collateral damage to athletes, who were given disproportionate, unfair, inconsistent sanctions with often limited or no routes to redemption, rehabilitation or career recovery. These issues are over-shadowed by evidence of organized and individual doping, which are most often used to justify the extension of WADA power and punishment of athletes, rather than being identified as a reason to reflect and initiate reforms.

This book considers how we arrived at this situation and asks what can be done to make the policy more reasonable through a range of adaptations, and especially how to engage athletes in the future improvement of anti-doping. We propose that athletes should be part of the system, not simply subject to it and treated with doubt and suspicion as potential cheats. Instead, we recognize that it is athletes who suffer the indignities of the anti-doping 'gaze' and the damage of harsh punishments to their careers and lives beyond sport. This engagement should not just be for a handful of cherrypicked athletes already known to WADA, the IOC and others – all athletes should be given the chance to have their say. The intensification of anti-doping since the 1990s has led to a power imbalance. We propose an approach based on cooperation, mutual respect, support for athletes before and after a doping violation and consideration of their circumstances. Proportionality, fairness and fundamental respect for the humanity of those impacted should be at the heart of anti-doping in the future.

But first, let's look at how we got here.

1

The Origins of Doping and Anti-Doping in Modern Sport

Sport as we now recognize it came into being during the late nineteenth century. Of course, there had been various forms of physical competition in a variety of cultures and civilizations before then. Some carried religious significance, or were associated with local holidays, while others were part of royal celebrations. There were also highly organized and competitive sporting events, such as the ancient Olympic Games. Some sports evolved from traditional games, while others are recent inventions. One change that had implications for doping, and later for anti-doping, was the idea of sport as a profession. Sport as a paid career rather than a vocation or hobby was not common or widely accepted until quite recently and has led to the development of new ways of thinking about and doing sport. Gaining celebrity and monetary rewards for sporting success was not new, but these shifts in sporting culture would have a dramatic effect in the twentieth century.

Britain became the crucible of world sport during the period of rapid urbanization and industrialization in the mid- to late nineteenth century. The shift from an agrarian economy to one focused around factories within towns and cities meant that time and space became highly structured. The notion of 'leisure' time spread among different social groups in these years. Clear boundaries between working and non-working hours impacted both the ways people organized their time and what was made available to them when off the clock. This differentiated work from play and opened up the consumer leisure industry.

Sports clubs became a new, popular part of British culture. Some developed to encourage participation and recreational sport. However, other clubs emerged with a competitive focus. Some of these elite clubs selected the best players to represent them and their community. This was helped along by new technologies that allowed for easier, quicker travel. The introduction of the rail system meant that teams could be formed and regularly play each other in leagues. In order to avoid conflicts over local rules, sports needed some common, formalized guidelines so that competitions would be controlled and fair. In turn, those rules needed governing bodies to ensure that the clubs followed them. Governing bodies undertook the standardization of how sports would be contested and officials were trained to ensure these policies were correctly implemented. By the 1870s and '80s, national tournaments and leagues had emerged and many more clubs were formed in a range of sports.[1]

Other countries were not far behind. The British Empire provided fertile ground for spreading these new rules and competition formats far beyond Britain and even continental Europe. The imperial diffusion of sport was driven by working-class soldiers and labourers who took their games abroad as pastimes when dispatched for long stretches. Equally important were colonial officers, teachers and religious leaders who used sport to discipline colonial subjects. The lessons of self-discipline, following orders and the gentlemanly handshake after the game were all considered important parts of British culture that should be instilled in the colonies. Sport provided a vehicle for teaching other values and lessons as well. Missionaries trying to Christianize and 'civilize' the locals also used sport within their schools and churches. The idealism of the English public-school system was combined with the Victorian theory of rational recreation to promote organized sports at home and abroad.

Of course, there were differences of class, gender and cultural identity inherently wrapped up in sporting cultures. The middle and upper classes played cricket, rugby and hockey; the lower classes played football and boxed. Clubs were often exclusionary: rules against membership for women, 'natives' and (working-class) professionals were common. Sport brought communities together in shared activities, but could also define, separate and distinguish groups within those communities as necessary.[2]

A commercial impetus sat alongside these amateur and moralistic endeavours. Many entrepreneurs seized the opportunity presented by this new appetite for mass entertainment. Club owners could charge entrance fees by restricting access to matches. Popular sports were covered in the media, which allowed for additional revenue streams by selling sponsorships and advertising. Team sports like football found huge pools of support due to their identification with specific towns and communities. These were often associated with specific factories or businesses that would give the workers a half-day off on Saturdays to watch their team play. This drove loyalty and interest, as well as provided opportunities for spending money. Local and national rivalries stoked interest in these matches and players soon became celebrities.

By the end of the century, sport saw the rise of a new type of sportsman: the professional athlete. Professionalism was rapidly accepted in sports such as football and cycling. Others were not so quick. Rugby league allowed players to be paid while rugby union did not (it was not until the early 1990s that rugby union was professionalized). There were other issues and implications of professionalism that some sports struggled to sort out. Prize money for athletics races became a source of tension between the traditionalists who wanted to keep athletics amateur and the progressives who felt athletes should be able to earn a living from their sporting labours. Many sports, not least horse racing, attracted gambling, leading to suspicions of race and match fixing. The rapid development of rules in a number of sports was intended partly to protect the fairness of competition for the athletes and teams, but also to protect bookmakers and gamblers from unfair practices on and off the field. The fledgling sports industry needed transparent rules and regulations.[3]

Indicative of the global scale and scope of this new sporting culture was the founding of the International Olympic Committee, formed in 1894, and the staging of the first modern Olympic Games in 1896 in Athens. The effort to hold a global multi-sport event was led by Baron Pierre de Coubertin, whose speeches and writings often referred to the lofty ideal of friendly competition. He was inspired by the English public-school approach to sport in the mid-nineteenth century. Central to this vision was amateurism: the strict rule that no athlete should get paid. Underpinning this idea was the belief that sport had a purity and nobility that would be lost, indeed corrupted, if money was changing hands. There was, of course, some class snobbery here. Competing in sport at a high level was time-consuming and expensive, especially when factoring in travel and time spent away from paid work. Wealthy people could afford to do sport purely for leisure, but less privileged athletes needed to earn money.

Some sports institutionalized this class division. Cricket had a clear distinction between Gentlemen and Players, which included the use of changing areas and pavilion spaces and the contributions they made to the team. The Olympics was designed for amateurs, meaning athletes had to be wealthy to participate, not least because the events took place in various countries and lasted several weeks. The 1981 Oscar-winning film *Chariots of Fire* epitomized this division. The film focused on the 1924 Olympic Games in Paris. Almost all the competitors were middle or upper class, including some who were students at Cambridge University. Events like these were the exclusive domain of those who could afford not to work. Money, rather than talent, likely decided many Olympic outcomes.

It is worthwhile to note that one of the main characters in *Chariots of Fire* was based on Lord Burghley, who would be at the forefront of the IOC's first official decree against the use of drugs in sport in 1938. A less prominent character was New Zealander Arthur Porritt. Porritt eventually moved to England, became a royal physician and was tasked with leading the IOC's first Medical Commission in 1961. The Commission's remit included developing anti-doping rules and testing.

Early Experiments

The earliest documented examples of early drug use in high-level sport are from the 1904 and 1908 Olympic Games, and both involved strychnine and marathon runners. There had been one major case of alleged drug use before then: the death of cyclist Arthur Linton in 1896. His death has been widely attributed to doping. A Welsh champion, Linton often competed in the major European races. His coach, James Edward 'Choppy' Warburton, had a reputation for giving his riders a secret concoction to drink. When Linton died after the Bordeaux–Paris race, it seemed plausible that stimulant drugs were at least partly to blame. This myth was repeated in a broad range of publications throughout the twentieth century. Linton's actual death, however, was far less dramatic, though no less tragic. His *Times* obituary indicated that the talented cyclist died several weeks after the race from typhoid.[4] The repetition of his alleged death-by-doping tragedy demonstrates how drug use captured the imagination of many writers: the idea that someone would take such high risks and suffer such serious consequences for sporting success contains all the ingredients for a captivating drama.

There are other relatively innocuous examples of runners and cyclists using stimulants around the time of Linton's death. Cocaine had become widely available and was rumoured to be popular among long-distance cyclists. The marketing of coca (from leaves) and cola (from nuts) in tonic drinks led to the creation of Coca-Cola, while cocaine was widely sold in drinks, pills and powders for use as pain relievers and 'pep pills'. Far from pushing the boundaries of enhancement, athletes were simply following trends. Scientists had been showing the value of these substances since the 1870s. One of the earliest experiments on coca leaves took place in Edinburgh in 1870 and 1875, led by Sir Robert Christison, professor of medicine at the University of Edinburgh, Ordinary Physician to the Queen in Scotland and president of the British Medical Association. He used his first batch in 1870 to assess the effects on two students who walked 16 miles with no stimulant. When they

Arthur Linton, falsely accused of being the first doping death.

returned in a state of exhaustion, he gave each a small amount of coca, which re-energized them enough to continue walking for another hour. Five years later, Christison experimented on himself on three occasions: twice on local walks, and once while hiking the 985-metre Ben Vorlich mountain in Scotland. He was 78 years old at the time. He reported feeling less tired when he took the coca towards the end of the first walk of 15 miles. For the mountain hike, he used the drug only towards the end of the ascent, around 100 metres from the summit. In fact, he was full of praise for the effects and the lack of side effects. Reflecting on the hillwalking experience in the *British Medical Journal*, he wrote: 'I at once felt that all fatigue was gone, and I went down the long descent with an ease like that which I used to enjoy in my mountainous rambles in my youth.' He felt 'neither weary, nor hungry, nor thirsty, and felt as if I could easily walk home four miles'.[5]

Sir Robert Christison, who conducted experiments on coca leaves in the 1870s.

Sigmund Freud wrote about coca in 1884, based on his own use and accounts he had heard from other users. He 'professed optimism about its potential to counteract nervous debility, indigestion, cachexia, morphine addiction, alcoholism, high-altitude asthma, and impotence'.[6] Coca was seen as having the potential to cure a range of ills rather than being the cause of them. By the early twentieth century cocaine was widely consumed. Of course, this was before its addictive properties were generally known. Historians George Andrews and David Solomon described the situation in America:

> Anybody could saunter into a drug store and buy cocaine in a variety of forms. Indeed, it appeared in so many guises that the druggist might well have asked the customer whether it was wanted to be sniffed as a powder, nibbled as a bonbon, sucked as a lozenge, smoked as a coca-leaf cigarette, rubbed on the skin as an ointment, used as a painkilling gargle, inserted into bodily cavities as a suppository, or drunk as a thirst-quenching beverage such as Coca-Cola.[7]

Other substances were equally attractive to early researchers of performance enhancement. Scientists in several countries researched the effects of food, vitamins, drinks and stimulant drugs on sport performance in various contexts. For example, in the late nineteenth century the leading French scientist Philippe Tissié used an elite cyclist to study the properties of potentially stimulating drinks. Also in France, the psychologist Gustave Le Bon was interested in discovering the effects of the kola nut. Le Bon experimented on a leading cyclist, concluding that the nut was a 'powerful resource'. Before long, kola as well as coca garnered much interest from scientists and manufacturers of tonics, medicines and supplements. Both were new to North America and Europe after being imported from South America.

The 1904 Olympic Games were held in St Louis in the United States. As usual, the marathon race was one of the main attractions. The event ended up being overshadowed by scandal after attempts by American Fred Lorz to cheat his way to success by being driven in a car for part of the route. His disqualification meant that his rival, Thomas Hicks, won the race. In those days the marathon was a rather brutal affair and the 1904 race was no exception. Runners had support staff in cars and ran in very unforgiving footwear. The summer heat in St Louis meant that temperatures were over 32°C (90°F). There was only one water station on the course, as the science of hydration was newly emergent. Of the 32 runners who started, only fourteen finished. Hicks suffered greatly for his win. In order to get him across the finish line, Hicks was dosed with strychnine mixed with brandy during the race. Late twentieth-century descriptions suggest that he collapsed at the finish and nearly died, likely because of the strychnine. Whether because of this or the unforgiving conditions, Hicks was in poor shape following the marathon.

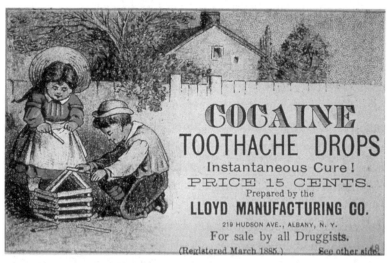

Example of the everyday use of cocaine in the late 19th and early 20th centuries.

Thomas Hicks, winner of the 1904 Olympic marathon, with the winner's trophy.

As with the Linton story, a near-suicide-for-gold-medals story is so attractive to writers that many have failed to consult the historical evidence or examine the broader social context. At the time, strychnine was not strictly considered a poison and scientists investigated its stimulant properties alongside its risks. For example, scientific research presented to the Royal College of Physicians in 1906 concluded that strychnine reduced fatigue. More specifically, a paper in the *Journal of Physiology* in 1908 showed that a few milligrams given orally produced 'an increase in the capacity for muscular work' which peaked between thirty minutes and three hours after ingestion, according to the dose, and thereafter capacity became subnormal. Doctors lauded strychnine for its medical properties in this era. The medical historian John S. Haller Jr wrote that by the end of the nineteenth century the drug had become 'one of the most powerful in the physician's medical handbag'.[8]

In the context of scientific research into stimulants, the description provided by Dr Charles Lucas, who both authored the official Olympic Report and accompanied Hicks as his trainer on the course, is worthy of consideration. He wrote that the use of strychnine helped Hicks to win the race as his opponents lacked 'proper care on the road'. He explained that Hicks had been 'kept in mechanical action by the use of drugs'. For Lucas, the race had 'demonstrated that drugs are of much benefit to athletes along the road'. This was the application of science to sport, and there was no reason not to do so. Lucas described Hicks as having 'the greatest honour ever brought to American shores by an American athlete'.

We can compare this to the reaction across the Atlantic to the use of a much less artificial aid to performance – extra oxygen. Supplemental oxygen had been publicly discussed in reference to a Scottish swimmer called Jabez Wolffe. Between 1906 and 1913 he made 22 unsuccessful attempts to swim the English Channel. The closest Wolffe came was in 1908, when he failed by only yards. During that attempt he was given oxygen. It is not clear exactly how, but it was likely administered using a diving mask connected to a pressurized tank carried on a boat. His closest rival, Montague Holbein, who was also unsuccessful in his attempts, criticized this form of performance enhancement as unsportsmanlike. However, one fascinating culturally loaded criticism came from the English aristocrat Lord Lonsdale. He was an avid sportsman: his name is still associated with boxing, but he was also chairman of Arsenal Football Club and the first president of the

Automobile Association. Lonsdale inherited vast wealth and property, most of which he squandered on failed sporting ventures. He was quoted in the *New York Times* as saying that Wolffe's use of oxygen was 'unsportsmanlike and un-English'.

At the risk of over-simplifying or indulging in crude stereotyping, doping was culturally more acceptable within environments where scientific knowledge and progress were useful for work, war and play. In England, the restrictions of tradition and scepticism over modern notions of rational progress – combined with long-established class-based ideas about sport – created suspicion around the use of artificial forms of performance enhancement. Indeed, the first doping rules we know about were established in 1908 at the London Olympics.

The Birth of Anti-Doping

Although we have no evidence of contemporary criticism of Thomas Hicks, Charles Lucas or the use of strychnine, something prompted the organizers and the IOC to include a rule for the London 1908 Olympic Games. This new rule applied only to the marathon and specified that the use of any drug would lead to disqualification. However, the rule was almost laughably unenforceable. It did not define what was or was not considered a drug, and, of course, there was no form of scientific testing to detect covert use. Moreover, a later section of the marathon rules explains what sustenance would be made available to the runners (possibly also in response to the deprivations of the 1904 race), and clearly says that stimulants can be used for recovery purposes. A surprising aspect of this section of the rules is the lack of clarity as to what constitutes recovery (as opposed to performance enhancement), especially considering what had happened with Hicks just four years prior.[9] The rule did not apply to any other event, so presumably athletes in other disciplines could use any drug they liked.

The new rule did little to stop the runners using strychnine. Its use in the 1908 race was less public, but there was a different kind of controversy around that year's event. The Italian runner Dorando Pietri became a global celebrity as a result of his own strychnine scandal. Pietri was a leading contender for the gold medal, having completed a marathon in just over two and half hours in preparation for the Games. The event took place in hot conditions and the athletes again struggled in the later stages. Pietri was given strychnine as a stimulant. Despite that, or possibly because of it, he fell several times in the final 2 kilometres of the race and received help to recover and continue. He was so disoriented upon arriving at the stadium that he started to run in the wrong direction around the track. He was first over the line, but it took him ten minutes to complete the final 350 metres. Nevertheless, 75,000 people cheered as he eventually reached the tape. Unfortunately for Pietri, the assistance he received to finish was illegal and he was disqualified. The gold medal was instead awarded to American Johnny Hayes.

Dorando Pietri being aided during the marathon
at the 1908 Olympic Games.

Baron Pierre
de Coubertin,
founder of the
modern Olympic
Games.

The race doctors knew about his apparent doping infringement, stating that Pietri took a 'dope of strychnine and atropia' and nearly died. Far from being disgraced for either doping or being helped in the final stages, he was in fact acclaimed by all and sundry. The IOC president Baron Pierre de Coubertin wrote, 'The disqualification of Dorando Pietri, winner of the marathon, infuriated popular opinion. No one can dispute the fact that Dorando was the moral winner of the competition.' Queen Alexandra gave him a special prize of a silver cup. De Coubertin saw this as reflective of 'the unanimous sentiment of the nation'. Sherlock Holmes author Arthur Conan Doyle wrote in a local paper that Pietri should be honoured in such a way.[10] He then raised money for Pietri to start a bakery business in his hometown. His fame grew such that Irving Berlin wrote a song for him simply titled 'Dorando'. Pietri embarked on a racing tour in the USA. He won seventeen out of 22 races, including two against Johnny Hayes, one of which was held at Madison Square Garden in New York City.

Doping was hardly a major issue in world sport at this point. There are almost no known significant incidents that demonstrate that drug use was considered to be unethical or unhealthy in the period up to the Second World War. More broadly, there was growing interest in expanding human potential, especially that of labourers. In traditional industry and manufacturing, the search for increasing productivity focused attention on fatigue reduction and the optimization of workers' output on the back of Taylorist time-and-motion studies. Assembly line processes broke down the production of goods like cars into discrete tasks to improve efficiency. This allowed workers to work longer hours on specific tasks. The rise of the professional athlete coincided with this rise of 'scientific manufacturing'. In many ways the principles were similar: sporting success depended on moving the body with the most efficient and effective motions; manufacturing processes in craft industries were broken down into individual tasks that could be completed more efficiently via a production line.[11]

In the 1920s and '30s experimental studies on the effects of a variety of substances on performance were on the rise. Some of these would later feature prominently in the doping crisis of the post-war period. Studies of amphetamines and other similar stimulants were already underway, as were early experiments with hormonal therapies.[12] The amphetamine Benzedrine was produced and sold by Smith, Kline & French as a decongestant inhaler by the early 1930s. Scientists in Europe and North America concentrated on leveraging the potential of such stimulants across a range of applications. Again, the focus of this research was not necessarily aimed at sport.

Around this time a rather unusual situation emerged in English football. In 1925 the manager of Arsenal, Leslie Knighton, gave his players 'pep pills' before two important FA Cup matches against local rivals West Ham United. The exact contents of these pills are unknown, as this incident pre-dates the wide-scale availability of amphetamines. Knighton had received them from a neighbour who was a 'distinguished West End doctor', a keen supporter of the club who had visited him specifically to propose the use of stimulants for the West Ham match. Knighton recounted the doctor's argument:

> What the boys require is something in the nature of a courage-pill. Occasionally, we administer such things to patients requiring abnormal stamina or resistance for a particular purpose. They do no harm, but simply tone up the nerve reflexes to produce the maximum effort, and they leave no serious after-effects.[13]

Knighton agreed to give the pills a try. He enthusiastically described the effects of the drugs on the players and himself, 'Just before kick-off time I saw that the boys were getting restless. So was I. I felt I needed to run, jump, shout. There was something in those pills. I felt I could push down a wall with my fist.' For the match on 10 January, in an absurd twist, the players were all pepped up and ready to go when the match was cancelled due to thick fog. Knighton then faced a different challenge, 'Getting the boys back to Highbury that afternoon was like trying to drive a flock of lively young lions.' The physical effects were hyperactivity as well as dehydration that left a dry, bitter thirst not easily quenched with glasses of water.

However, they persevered and used the pills again in the rescheduled match two days later on 12 January. Knighton colourfully described the 'agonies of thirst and violent restlessness'. But the impact on the field of play overrode these side effects. The players 'seemed like giants suddenly supercharged'; they 'tore away with the ball, and put in shots that looked like leather thunderbolts'. Even in the second half, the players 'ran like Olympic sprinters behind the ball, jumped like rockets to reach the high ones, and crashed in shots from all angles and distances'. Though they failed to score and the match ended in a draw, Knighton was very happy with the stimulants. His summation was that West Ham 'had no defence against the pluck-pills'.

Curiously, the players did not feel the same way. When the manager produced the box with pills just before the next match they rebelled and refused to take them. The match ended with a 2–2 draw and left Knighton with a strong sense of regret: 'Our play was not nearly so determined as it had been in the former game, and I believe we should have netted two more goals if the pills had been taken.' The tie was finally settled in the next game in favour of West Ham, with Knighton's players again refusing to take the pep pills. The manager was rueful: 'I often wondered if we should have won if the boys doped for that game. Just a bit of extra pep when we were so often pressing the West Ham defence . . . We did not lose when we took the pills, and did not win when we rejected them. I wonder?'[14]

Although this episode was not publicized at the time, the fact that the full story appeared in Knighton's 1948 autobiography indicates there was a general tolerance, if not acceptance, of stimulant use in professional sport even up until the late 1940s. If a leading manager thought it acceptable to record this, we might conclude that he was not too anxious about attracting criticism. Moreover, the role of the anonymous doctor is fascinating: he was apparently undeterred by medical ethics and motivated by his support for the team. Similar situations might have been common in football or other sports, but there are few, if any, historical accounts with as many details as this story.

Just over a decade later, the use of amphetamines in football was more pronounced, although the ambiguities around drug use were clear. Though they were still used, there was a vague sense of disquiet in a context of slowly emerging prohibition. A trainer called Tom Whittaker complained in the *News of the World* in 1938 that the 'new drug, Benzedrine ... has the effect of pepping-up sluggish players and may succeed in rousing the spirit of men and women who are only at their best when they are on the verge of losing their temper. It is stronger than aspirin and caffeine, and brings about a reaction afterwards, although it is not the type of drug to which one becomes addicted.' He admitted that it could create 'performances of unbelievable brilliance'. Yet he was wary of the issues, writing, 'But at what cost of human suffering! That would be the end of sport as we understand it.' It is unclear why Whittaker continued on to criticize long-term use, arguing that 'one is inclined to get fed up with it. I regard it as dangerous in the long run.'[15] Articles like this indicate that stimulant use in the 1930s was common while also hinting at the coming debates that would forge anti-doping policy in the post-war period. The article was sensationally headlined: 'Will Science Give Us ROBOT ATHLETES?'

A more balanced approach was clear in the work of scientist Ove Bøje. In 1939 he wrote a detailed summary of such studies in a paper entitled 'Doping' for the *Bulletin of the Health Organization of the League of Nations*. He highlighted the potential of amphetamines for improving performance and reflected on the ethical debate by arguing that doping seemed no different to having a coach or psychologist support athletes as they sought to improve their chances of success. Two years later, Peter Karpovich, a professor of physiology at Springfield College in Massachusetts and one of the founding members of the American College of Sports Medicine (ACSM, in 1954), published a review article in the *Research Quarterly* of the American Physical Education Association. He summarized studies on nineteen 'ergogenic aids': alcohol, alkalines, ammonium chloride, Benzedrine, caffeine, cocaine, nikethemide, digitalis, gelatin and glycine, fruit juices, hormones, lecithin, metrazol, oxygen, phosphates, sodium chloride, sugars, ultraviolet rays and vitamins. The outcomes were a mixed bag of evidence and speculation. He claimed that alcohol was useful for warming up the body prior to physical activity but could be detrimental to performance. Benzedrine was treated with caution; while research showed it could counteract fatigue, he warned that 'it is a powerful and dangerous drug and its excess may lead to insomnia, hypertonia, and circulatory collapse.' Cocaine was similarly considered risky for its dangerous and addictive qualities. Curiously, he claimed that the consensus medical opinion was that caffeine should be prohibited in sport.

Yet Karpovich also provided a fascinating insight into the cultural contexts for these scientific commentaries. He raised a number of concerns about social attitudes, behaviours and the risks of enhancing substances:

> In facing a situation where a rapid increase in physical fitness is of great importance, several questions immediately present themselves: Are there any special foodstuffs, drugs, or any other means which will increase work capacity? What are they? Are they dangerous? Newspapers, and even scientific periodicals, from time to time carry articles describing the remarkable effect of various 'aids', which are able to increase muscular strength and the speed of movements, and delay the onset of fatigue, thus improving endurance. In most cases, a wave of enthusiasm affects the would-be investigators of these 'aids', and the result is poorly controlled experiments which unfortunately support the original work, when that work in itself may be questionable. Critical and contradictory articles soon appear, but as usual, the negative findings are slower in affecting the practical field, and the

impetus gained by the 'positive' observations may prevail for a long time, especially if supported by commercial interest.[16]

Despite his concerns, Karpovich did not propose regulation or prohibition. The normal cycle of knowledge, experiments and criticism seemed to be the framework in which he understood doping. He argued that any substance that improves performance without risking the health of the user should be considered ethical. Nor was it unethical or unsportsmanlike to gain an advantage over a sporting rival using these substances, as such performance aids were widely available to athletes and not dissimilar to other training methods, dietary improvements and physiotherapy. Therefore, what we see in Karpovich and other scientists' approach is a realistic and pragmatic acceptance that athletes were seeking out means to enhance their performance. Research, then, could provide a solid basis for them to understand the benefits and risks – what we might now understand as a harm reduction approach to doping.

As early as the 1920s, the competing ideologies over doping were playing out in amateur and professional sports. The historians John Gleaves and Matthew Llewellyn made this clear distinction in their review of early twentieth-century doping:

> Nonetheless, turn-of-the-century professional sport proved much more accepting of drugs. In part, the de facto class-divide separating working-class professionals and gentleman amateurs allowed professional athletes the freedom to use stimulants free from amateur sport's 'moralizing' influence. Professional sports such as boxing, pedestrianism and cycling openly permitted athletes to use stimulants as needed from the 1890s to the 1910s.[17]

Professional sports were slow to react to the criticisms related to drug use in the 1920s and '30s. Although evidence is sparse, there were rumours about cyclists using cocaine and amphetamines. In the absence of consistent anti-doping condemnation or regulation, scientists openly discussed the potential value of substances and were not restricted in their experimental designs. Openness and transparency were acceptable moderators for these trials. However, Gleaves and Llewellyn made the case that there was a key difference in who was allowed to dope. Once again, the divide was along social class lines, and the Olympics became a focal point for broader social divisions:

> For the 'lower classes', sport was not a means of leisure but a means for economic profit and entertainment. Using sport for such purposes precluded these individuals from realising the middle- and upper-classes notions about sport's moral purpose. Indeed, the tacit tolerance of doping in professional sport permitted upper class social groups to delegitimise the professional athletic performances among those from less powerful social status.[18]

In 1928 we saw the beginnings of formal anti-doping led by Sigfrid Edström, a Swedish industrialist and former 100-metre sprinter who was president of the IOC from 1946 to 1952 and honorary president from 1952 to 1964. He first held a position within the IOC in 1920, becoming vice-president in 1931. He was a committed amateur who famously supported the ban on the Finnish athlete Paavo Nurmi competing at the 1932 Olympics on the basis that he was a professional. Edström's involvement with the Olympics included organizing the 1912 Games in Stockholm. During those Games, the IAAF was established and Edström was elected president, a position he held until 1946.

The IAAF strengthened its position on amateurism in 1928, formalizing rules that its members could not receive prize money or appearance fees. At the same time, its executive council proposed the first organizational rule prohibiting drug use, which was unanimously accepted by its Congress. The wording of this rule was strategic, as it would influence the IOC's stance, not least through Edström's joint roles:

> Doping is the use of any stimulant not normally employed to increase the power of action in athletic competition above the average. Any person knowingly acting or assisting as explained above shall be excluded from any place where these rules are in force or, if he is a competitor, be suspended for a time or otherwise, from participation in amateur athletics under the jurisdiction of this Federation.[19]

Considering how historically important this rule would become, there was very little response from the international sports media or other sports organizations at the time. Yet it is clear in the above that the concept of doping was vague and subjective from its earliest inception. It is also unlikely that agreed definitions could be found for 'normally employed', 'above the average' or for what sort of punishments should be associated with 'suspended for a time or otherwise'.

It would take ten years for the IOC to signal its intent to support the IAAF's anti-doping position. In between, the debate continued about the nature of stimulants and their potential harms. An example of this came from an outspoken critic of drug use, the German scientist Otto Reisser, who was director of the Pharmacological Institute of the University of Breslau. He undertook a review of potentially useful substances for enhancing sporting performance, and concluded that phosphates, caffeine, theobromine and chocolate were beneficial in this regard. However, he held strong misgivings about how such substances should be used in sport. With these concerns in mind, he addressed the German Swimming Federation in 1933:

The use of artificial means [to improve performance] has long been considered wholly incompatible with the spirit of sport and has therefore been condemned. Nevertheless, we all know that this rule is continually being broken, and that sportive competitions are often more a matter of doping than of training. It is highly regrettable that those who are in charge of supervising sport seem to lack the energy for the campaign against this evil, and that a lax, and fateful, attitude is spreading. Nor are the physicians without blame for this state of affairs, in part on account of their ignorance, and in part because they are prescribing strong drugs for the purpose of doping which are not available to athletes without prescriptions.[20]

The Olympic movement formally took a stance against doping in 1938. It was deeply interwoven with the protection of amateurism. The president of the IOC at this time was the Belgian aristocrat Henri de Baillet-Latour, who had taken over from de Coubertin and held the position from 1925 until 1942. His presidential legacy has been largely overshadowed by the decision in spring 1939 to allow Germany to host the 1940 Winter Olympics (which was subsequently reversed two months after Germany invaded Poland). Yet Baillet-Latour was also known for his commitment to protecting amateurism. In 1937 he offered a strong opinion on the relationship of sports values and drug use: 'amateur sport is meant to improve the soul and the body, therefore no stone must be left unturned as long as the use of doping has not been stamped out.' He was supported by other members of the IOC, who were each from the elite strata of society, notably Sigfrid Edström, American Avery Brundage (a staunch amateur supporter who would become IOC president from 1952 to 1972), the Italian aristocrat Count Alberto Bonacossa and German Karl Ritter von Halt (a high-ranking sports official who would be president of the German Olympic Committee 1952–60). Another contributor with passionate anti-doping views was the Englishman Lord David Burghley, Marquess of Exeter. He was a successful athlete who competed at the 1924, 1928 and 1932 Olympics, winning the gold for the 400-metre hurdles in 1928 and silver in the 400-metre relay in 1932. He was born into wealth and educated at the Institut Le Rosey in Switzerland, Eton College and the University of Cambridge, where he was president of the Cambridge University Athletic Club. He was the archetypal gentleman amateur. Among other sports leadership roles, he would become the IAAF president in 1946. Again, the links between social class, amateur ideals and doping were clear among the IOC leadership.

The period 1936–8 would be formative for the IOC's stance on doping following reports to the IOC from doctors and evidence of drug use in various sports. In 1937 Avery Brundage expressed his opinion on the matter: 'The use of drugs or artificial stimulants of any kind cannot be too strongly denounced and anyone receiving or administering dope or artificial stimulants should be excluded from participation in sport or the O.G. [Olympic Games].'[21] The outcome of these IOC discussions was an announcement in 1938 in the IOC's *Bulletin*: 'The use of drugs or artificial stimulants of any kind must be condemned most strongly, and everyone who accepts or offers dope, no matter in what form, should not be allowed to participate in amateur meetings or in the Olympic Games.'[22]

Although it did not have an immediate effect, the idea that sport was not a place for drug use took shape in the 1920s and became formalized at the highest levels of international amateur sport by the late 1930s. This was not a dramatic shift in attitudes, since there were earlier indications of anti-drug sentiment in previous decades. However, there were specific social and cultural patterns forming around the time of these early regulations. First, the policy directives were coming from the organizations that led amateur sports, namely the IAAF and the IOC. Despite evidence and rumours surrounding football players and cyclists, there is no indication of public statements or policies from any organization representing professional or team sports. Doping remained an issue situated at the divide between amateurs and professionals.

Second, and related to this, doping also represented modernity. It was promoted by researchers interested in progressing new knowledge, pharmaceutical companies keen to innovate, manufacture and sell their products and doctors who embraced chemical interventions, and was used by professionals who were motivated by personal glory and money. Within the debates surrounding anti-doping and amateurism, ideas of purity and even the word 'clean' were juxtaposed with 'artificial'. Simply the presence of these professionals was a threat. Underlying this was, of course, the fear that professional sport could overwhelm and destroy amateur sport and the upper classes' dominance of it, and in doing so would undermine the values and ethics of sport. The IOC would not abandon the rule excluding professionals from competing at the Olympics until the 1970s.

Third, and less clearly, there were cultural differences. Many upper-class English amateur sportsmen such as Lord Lonsdale and Lord Burghley had strong anti-doping views, with the former, as we have seen, calling doping 'un-English'. Upper-class Europeans, not least Baillet-Latour, were also vocal in their opposition to the encroaching threat of professional athletes. By contrast, Charles Lucas had praised the use of drugs in the 1904 marathon. Similarly, working-class footballers, marathon runners and cyclists in many countries seemed to have no moral problem with drugs.

Doping was profoundly shaped by factors associated with class, power and notions of amateur versus professional sports. The meaning of doping was, then, socially constructed. The drugs themselves were not well understood, but side effects were not really a significant concern at the time. It was the potential for enhancing performance above and beyond what could be achieved by an athlete relying on their natural talents and dedication to their sport that was emerging as the central issue. Doping cut to the very heart of what sport meant, the power struggle between two opposing views. The dichotomy was obvious: dirty, artificial, professional, working class as opposed to clean, natural, amateur, middle/upper class. Somewhere between these juxtapositions was the media. Sporting contests and excellent achievements created good copy. The gossip and scandal of the 'dark side' of sport made even better copy. Winning was praised; winning through cheating received the most damning criticism.

These tensions would underpin the doping/anti-doping debate throughout the twentieth century and into the twenty-first, when policy changes emerged in social contexts only partially related to the actual pharmaceuticals involved.

2

Speed and Steroids

The dilemmas around doping had been seeping into sports organizations and media coverage during the interwar period, with science and class ideologies interwoven as inconsistent but visible threads. New knowledge meant opportunity. Entrepreneurialism and performance enhancement opened up pathways to stimulant use and led to resistance from those who sought to protect traditional amateur sport values and who feared excessive medicalization of sport. These competing forces came together in the late 1940s and led to an open debate about the role of drugs in sport in the 1950s. By the 1960s powerful drugs – anabolic-androgenic steroids – were changing athletes' bodies and abilities. Or, to put it another way, steroids were giving athletes the means and opportunity to improve their performance: taking sport to its logical next step. While anti-doping idealists sought to require athletes be to 'pure' and 'natural', the rest of society was open to the chemicalization of mind and body.

Amphetamines

In the immediate post-war period, there were no prohibitions on drug use in sport and a broad cultural acceptance of stimulants prevailed in many countries. One of the lesser-known aspects of the Second World War was that it acted as a catalyst for research into stimulants and for growing awareness of their benefits for the masses on a global scale. Rather than just supporting factory workers and athletes, scientists researching fatigue and how to reduce it were central to the war effort on both sides. Amphetamines and methamphetamines became widely used during the war years.

In 1938 the methamphetamine Pervitin was produced by the German pharmaceutical company Temmler, which had succeeded in developing a method of converting ephedrine into methamphetamine. This powerful central nervous system stimulant had the potential to impact the outcome of the war. In September 1939 the drug was brought to the attention of Otto Ranke, a military doctor and director of the Institute for General and Defence Physiology at Berlin's Academy of Military Medicine. He conducted a short experiment on ninety university students and concluded that Pervitin could be of great benefit to soldiers. The results of this trial were dramatic and use within the military was soon normalized. As Nicolas Rasmussen noted in his wide-ranging history of the drug:

> In the Blitzkrieg's opening months, German troops were widely issued the drug. Pervitin proved popular among Hitler's fighting men: the German military consumed 35 million methamphetamine tablets in April, May, and June 1940, the peak season of the Blitz. There were no orders from Berlin to use it in any particular way, so this consumption reflects demand among the soldiers and medics at the front.[1]

Similar patterns were emerging on the other side of the world. Japanese troops were given methamphetamines under the trade name Philopon, produced by Dainippon Pharmaceuticals. It has been estimated that 1 billion Philopon pills were produced between 1939 and 1945. This had a dramatic effect on public consumption after the war ended, as it proved a popular drug across Japanese society.

British military forces also embraced amphetamine use for wartime purposes. Several research studies were conducted in the early 1940s, and the Navy, Air Force and Army used the drug to combat physical and mental fatigue. Rasmussen's summary of British use indicates that it mirrored that of the Germans:

> British military demand for amphetamine – Benzedrine from SKF – was substantial, amounting to a wartime total of 72 million tablets. Since military personnel were forbidden to use the drug on British soil without special permission around the time the Air Ministry and Middle East Forces officially adopted amphetamine, this consumption represents use in combat theatres almost entirely.[2]

The good press received during the war worked to promote these drugs as a way of countering fatigue, which led to a rapid uptake after the war. Most countries had no legal restrictions on amphetamines or methamphetamines until the 1970s or '80s. Rather, they became associated with a wider range of benefits: reducing tiredness for long-distance drivers, shift workers and students cramming for exams and acting as appetite suppressants to encourage weight loss.

The wartime research and use of stimulants paved the way for an important and fascinating period in the history of stimulant use and anti-doping anxieties. Drugs that were commonly used in social life were inevitably making their way into sporting environments. Some professional athletes accepted the arrival of these drugs. Indeed, many saw new opportunities for improving their competitive performance and their chances of career success. There were no rules to prevent them from doing so, and the governing bodies of the main commercialized sports at this time were in no great rush to push forward policies that would prohibit their use. Some amateur athletes indulged in stimulant use as well. Again, there was no formal rule against it – the 1938 statement from the 10C against doping was not a formal rule – or any social reason not to (except for vague disapproval from some high-level sports administrators). However, by the late 1950s and into the early '60s there were competing perspectives on this issue from users, scientists and policy-makers both within and outside of sport that eventually led to a more formal approach from leading sport organizations.

The introduction of amphetamines into sport during the post-war period was the result of continued sales of the drugs in many countries and an ongoing sense of the positive value of their properties. Before long, there were examples of these types of drugs being used in American college sports, boxing, football, athletics and cycling, although evidence is patchy and episodic. The earliest instance of controversy surrounding stimulant use at the post-war Olympics came during the 1948 Summer Games held in London. The physician Christopher Woodward was a medical adviser to the British team and wrote this account for *Cycling* magazine, which was then picked up and repeated in the *New York Times*:

> I became suspicious that some competitors were receiving artificial stimulants at the Olympic Games. Two or three weeks later I was able to see things at closer range at the world cycling championships at Amsterdam, where I spent most of my time on the inside of the track. Few other than our own team knew who I was. Imagine my surprise therefore when a garrulous foreigner surreptitiously tried to show me his pet concoction of strychnine, caffeine and Benzedrine ... [drug use in sport] is more widespread than people think ... I've just visited Sweden and people there told me it was going on constantly.[3]

It is interesting to note the subtext of the suspicion, bordering on xenophobia, in the description of the 'garrulous foreigner' who was acting 'surreptitiously'. It is not dissimilar to Lord Lonsdale's comment that doping was 'un-English'. This is one of the earliest examples of stated concerns about stimulants at the Olympics. Four years later, a sports doctor would complain about the syringes he found in the athletes' changing rooms at the 1952 Helsinki Games. Quite how widespread such practices were is difficult to decipher from the snippets of evidence we have, most of which are observational rather than confessional.

However, further evidence was provided by an American sports doctor called Max Novich, who was open about his fellow Americans' drug use. Novich told a conference in 1964:

> Following the return of the [military] veteran to college, the use of amphetamine 'pep pills' became quite common among professional and intercollegiate athletes. Since the high school athlete and coach are influenced by the professional and intercollegiate athletes, the amphetamines became popular even in interscholastic athletics.[4]

Reflecting on this context, Sir Arthur Gold, a British sports administrator who would become prominent in anti-doping circles in the 1970s, was less forgiving. He essentially blamed the American sport environment for instigating doping, writing that it was here that 'the abuse of drugs in sport began on a substantial basis', the reasons being strongly related to the precarious nature of coaching employment:

> Sport was largely in the hands of Universities and high schools and the coaches, who are rather like football [soccer] managers but even less secure, were usually employed on a one year contract. A successful team, and they were

re-employed – an unsuccessful team and they joined the dole queue . . . and since most of their competitors were virtually in the same position as their employees, and were expendable, they didn't hesitate to introduce drug abuse into sport in the USA.[5]

Taken together, the accounts from Novich and Gold suggest that the war left a legacy of permissive attitudes towards amphetamines that were adopted in sports. Working conditions and job insecurity in sport increased demand for performance enhancement strategies. Broad social demand led to increased production and use of amphetamines on a global scale.

Nicolas Rasmussen referred to the general 1950s anxieties around drug use as the context for anti-doping: 'Concern with amphetamine in professional sports began to rise simultaneously with concern about the drug problem on the streets and in the military.'[6] However, the normality and wider acceptability of use can be seen in the fact that an estimated 2 million amphetamine tablets per day were being sold to the public in 1945 as cures for depression or to help with dieting.[7] It is far from surprising that people in sport would seek these out to help with fatigue, anxiety or body weight – especially with the apparently benign notion of a 'pep pill'. If the difference between winning and losing can come down to whether one is 'on form' then it is perfectly rational to take what is being offered and indeed used by millions of other people. Even these initial concerns that amphetamines in other sections of society were becoming a widespread problem would not be enough to deter athletes from seeking the benefits of these drugs.

Such ambivalence was highlighted in a high-profile public debate about amphetamine use in sport in 1957 when a leading scientist claimed that the four-minute mile record might have been assisted by amphetamine use. Herbert Berger was an expert on drug addiction and a consultant to the United States Public Health Service. In June of that year he delivered a lecture at the conference of the American Medical Association (AMA). He claimed, much like Novich and Gold, that amphetamines were being widely and indiscriminately used by athletes and coaches across the USA in boxing and American football, and by athletes at high-school, collegiate and professional levels of competition. Berger's criticism focused on three main areas: first, that using amphetamines could lead to 'violent rapacious and criminal behaviour'; second, that doping for sport could lead to more serious drug addiction; and third, that sporting records, including the four-minute mile, were being broken by drug users.[8] The first two of these critiques relate to social issues, but the third was clearly sports-specific and foreshadowed later anti-doping policies. The way anti-doping would come to be defined and managed would focus as much on 'cheating' or 'artificial performance enhancement' as it would on health, criminality or addiction.

Berger's allegations were eye-catching given the attention paid to the breaking of this running barrier. There was no evidence that any of those athletes who successfully ran under four minutes during this period were taking advantage of stimulants. As is widely known, the first runner to achieve it was an English medical student, Roger Bannister, on 6 May 1954. Bannister was an amateur athlete who did not train full time or run long distances as part of his record-breaking effort. His training was influenced by new ideas, such as interval training, in which athletes would do spurts of sprinting between periods of slower running. Other athletes were making similar progress: Australian runner John Landy achieved the sub-four-minute mile just 46 days after Bannister had done so. There would have been a dramatic sense of shock and disappointment if the allegations of drug use were true. Even though there were no formal rules against it, such a revelation would have carried some vague sense of cultural transgression.

The response to Berger's statements was mixed. There was a sense of outrage from track and field athletes who still associated doping with professionalism and corruption. An example of such came from Ron Delany, who had won gold in the 1,500 metres in the 1956 Melbourne Olympics:

> The whole idea that drugs are being used is absurd and crazy. I have never used drugs to help me run and I don't know of anyone else who has, anywhere in the world. That includes the four-minute milers. Track and field is an amateur sport – a clean sport. I don't think anyone in it would want to pay such a price just to win a race or break a record.[9]

Other athletes had different stories. Judy-Joy Davies, an Australian swimmer who had competed at the 1948 and 1952 Olympics, said: 'Some of our champion swimmers fearlessly admit they take pep pills to help them shatter records.' Neville Scott, a middle-distance runner from New Zealand, said that during the 1956 Olympics 'it seemed certain some Olympic athletes were taking drugs.'[10]

Stories of amphetamine use in American sport also came to light. A high-school coach from Oklahoma admitted giving student athletes phosphate pills, justifying this by claiming that other high-school teams used them. Two American football players admitted using Benzedrine pills while playing for a team in Toronto in 1955. Fred Davies, team doctor for the Ottawa Rough Riders American football team, claimed that the top four Canadian teams gave pep pills to their players before and during matches.[11]

In the aftermath of the Berger speech, Adolphe Abrahams, brother of the Olympian Harold Abrahams, wrote a lengthy contribution to *The Times* in which he outlined the arguments for and against drug use in sport. The AMA also responded by setting up research studies to be run under the auspices of a group called the Committee on Amphetamines and Athletes. Meanwhile the ACSM also took an interest and conducted social surveys. It reported in 1958 that of 133 responses (from 'trainers, coaches and physicians' working in sports), 35 per cent said they had knowledge that amphetamines and derivatives were being used in sport, and 63 per cent of this cohort believed those drugs improved performance.[12]

Despite Arthur Gold's comments focusing on U.S. athletes, it is clear that amphetamines were being used widely. And contrary to the idea that they were used only by professionals, many stories emerged of Olympic athletes and other amateurs looking for the beneficial effects of artificial stimulants.

Gordon Pirie was an English long-distance runner who competed in the 5,000-metre and 10,000-metre events at the 1952, 1956 and 1960 Olympics. He won a silver medal in 1956. He was also the second winner of the BBC Sports Personality of the Year Award in 1955. He wrote a reflective account of his sporting experiences in 1961 called *Running Wild*. In this book, he recalled an incident from the 1960 Olympics in which he was approached by a 'well known' British doctor who offered him pep pills. When he declined, another doctor who was present said: 'You must be one of the few mugs left who doesn't.' Pirie witnessed other athletes using Benzedrine and described this as a 'serious problem' that 'springs mainly from the extreme nationalism now poisoning sport'. He went on to accuse other countries' athletes, notably those from Eastern European and Soviet states. He also made the sort of generic health scare claim that would soon become commonplace among anti-doping campaigners: 'I believe it is standard practice before a race in certain Iron Curtain countries. Sudden staggering performances quite out of keeping with known form can only be explained by the use of drugs, and I believe their frequent use has accounted for the short athletic careers of some fine athletes.'[13]

Some cycling accidents in this era were attributed to the misuse of amphetamines and the problem seemed to be growing rapidly.

In 1949 an unnamed cyclist was admitted to an Italian hospital with what a doctor described as 'amphetamine poisoning'. The athlete subsequently died. If this is true, it is likely to be the first death attributed to doping. The Arthur Linton tragedy is often held up as the first such case, but there is no evidence to support that claim. As we will see, an infamous post-war death also wrongly attributed to doping is that of Danish cyclist Knud Enemark Jensen during the 1960 Olympics.

This first drug-related death in sport has been largely overlooked. This may be because the historical record is so patchy that we still do not even have the unfortunate cyclist's name. However, we do know that cyclists were using these drugs as a normal part of their day-to-day lives. Legendary Italian champion Fausto Coppi admitted this was the case. Coppi won several major races, including the doubles of the Giro d'Italia and Tour de France in both 1949 and 1952. After his retirement, he said that many cyclists used amphetamines 'and those who say otherwise aren't worth talking to about cycling'. Of his own use, he confessed, 'Yes, whenever it was needed,' which was 'practically all the time'. Along similar lines, French cyclist Roger Rivière admitted to using a 'massive' dose of amphetamines when he broke the one-hour cycling record in 1959.

Around this time, the influential sports doctor Pierre Dumas was becoming aware of cyclists' permissive attitudes towards drug use, as well as the potential risks. He said: 'the cyclists took everything they were offered. It didn't matter what they took, as long as they believed in it.' In 1959 he intercepted a package of strychnine addressed to one of the teams competing in the Tour de France. A year later, Marcel Bidot, the French national team manager, said: 'Three-quarters of the riders are doped. I am well placed to know since I visit their rooms each evening during the Tour. I always leave frightened after these visits.' That same year, Dumas checked in on the eventual race winner Gastone Nencini and found him 'lying in his bed with a drip infusing primitive hormones into both arms – and smoking a cigarette'.[14]

Within European football, some players, managers and team doctors thought amphetamine use was perfectly acceptable. A survey of Italian players in 1961 showed that 36 per cent had taken such drugs to prepare for matches.[15] In England two cases were openly discussed in the media. In 1962 a lower-league team, Chippenham Town, had been given pep pills by their manager, who told the *Daily Mail*: 'These pills give the lads extra energy in the last twenty minutes of the game. I don't think it's unfair. It's open to anyone to buy them at the chemists, as I did.'[16]

The other significant episode occurred at Everton during the 1961–2 season, and the season they won the League Championship, 1962–3. Details emerged that the players were given the drug Drinamyl, otherwise known as purple hearts, and Benzedrine, before matches to help performance. The players then used the same drugs recreationally at parties. The *Sunday People* newspaper claimed that the drugs 'were made freely available, by certain club officials, to anyone in the team who wanted them. These officials actually supplied and distributed the drugs before matches and even during training sessions.' The team goalkeeper Albert Dunlop, who became addicted to the drugs and to alcohol, said that the players would take up to four pills before a game.[17] In response, the club's board members offered an explanation that highlights how normal it was to use amphetamines. They denied any direct involvement but said that taking the pills was 'entirely a matter of personal choice, and medically, we are told, these pills, in the quantities taken, could not possibly have had any harmful effects on any player'.[18]

A 1962 systematic review of research into amphetamines covered their potential application in a diverse set of circumstances. Scientists Bernard Weiss and Victor Laties wrote: 'There can be little doubt that amphetamine can produce a significant enhancement of athletic performance, even in events in which, like putting the shot, one cannot see where endurance or fatigue would play a major role.'[19] They also addressed the question of potential negative effects. In their conclusion, they argued that amphetamine is a 'rather benign agent'.[20] In fact, they concluded that it was more benign than caffeine. More specifically, they showed that amphetamine improves mood, does not impair judgement and was not considered to be addictive. It is small wonder it took off so quickly in the world of sport.

Steroids

The history of how anabolic steroids became part of world sport includes some curious tales that need to be treated with caution. It is well known that in the late nineteenth century the pioneering endocrinologist Charles-Édouard Brown-Séquard conducted experiments on himself using testicular extracts from guinea pigs and dogs. Steroid science stuttered through the interwar period with further ad hoc experimentation.

The 1936 Olympics were held in Berlin, and were later to be labelled the Nazi Games. In due course, it was rumoured that German athletes had been given steroids to boost their performance, an idea that has subsequently been shown to be entirely false. It is, of course, a symbolic idea in that it associates the corruption of the Olympics with Nazis, fascism and Hitler. Doping and evil are apparently easy to correlate.

Another apparent example is that of English football teams that reportedly administered monkey-gland treatments to their players in 1938. The tabloid media reported this with a sense of shock and scandal. However, there is limited evidence of any truth to these stories.[21]

A balanced scientific perspective on the topic was presented in Peter Karpovich's review of potential ergogenic substances in 1941 when he raised the notion that hormone therapies could plausibly increase levels of physical fitness but that further research was required.[22] Four years later, the controversial American scientist Paul de Kruif wrote the first book on the subject. He is best known for a seminal text reviewing the development of scientific knowledge on microbes published in 1926. He was subsequently fired from his post at the Rockefeller Institute for Medical Research after being unveiled as the anonymous author critical of doctors' knowledge and practices. In 1945 he published *The Male Hormone*, which was widely reviewed in the American media. The cover blurb summed up his argument:

The male hormone discloses magic far beyond the mere sexual. It boosts muscle power. It banishes mental fatigue. It eases heart pain. It even restores the sanity of men in middle life who suffer from physical deficiencies.

He made the connection between this new field of research (labelling scientists as 'hormone hunters') and sports performance:

We know both the St. Louis Cardinals and St. Louis Browns have won championships super-charged by vitamins. It would be interesting to watch the productive power of an industry or a professional group that would try a systematic supercharge with testosterone – of course under a good hormone hunter's supervision.[23]

In fact, there were scientific studies of hormone therapies underway at this time. In 1944 a group of American researchers gave six men methyltestosterone, supplied by the German pharmaceutical company Schering under the name Oreton-M, for three to six weeks. The results, published in the *Journal of Clinical Endocrinology*, confirmed de Kruif's supposition: 'enhancement of central nervous system reflex time, back strength muscle enhancement, and increases in dynamic and static work performance'.[24] In 1945 the u.s. magazine *Businessweek* proclaimed: 'Of all the sex hormones, testosterone is said to have the greatest market potential.'[25]

Despite de Kruif's book and early experiments, there is no evidence of steroid use in sport until the early 1950s, when we come across another strange point-of-origin story. In 1954 two sports doctors met for a drink during the world weightlifting championships in Vienna. One was John Ziegler, the u.s. team's medic and later the doctor for the Olympic squad. Ziegler had a successful career in medicine at this point, specializing in neurology and working part-time as a researcher for the pharmaceutical company Ciba. His involvement with strength sport athletes resulted from his own participation in bodybuilding at the York Barbell club, owned by pioneering strength sport expert and entrepreneur Bob Hoffman.

As a medical expert, Ziegler's involvement in the competitive world of weightlifting had developed as the sport became increasingly scientific and popular. By the late 1940s the rivalry between the usa and the ussr had begun to take on greater symbolic significance in the context of the Cold War. Who had the strongest men started to matter: it was a proxy for the Cold War, including the nuclear war that seemed ever more possible through the 1950s and '60s. This sporting rivalry came to be known as the 'Big Arms Race'. The doctor Ziegler met in Vienna was from the Soviet Union and apparently showed some curiosity about whether the American strongmen were using drugs to help build their bodies. When Ziegler denied that there was anything artificial going on, his counterpart allegedly confessed that his team was using testosterone.

If Ziegler was shocked by this news, he showed no signs of being ethically disturbed. After all, there was no big debate about doping; nor were there rules to say that dosing men with additional male hormones was anything other than good science. Given that the Soviets were one step ahead and there was no reason not to try to catch up, Ziegler took the information gleaned from his loquacious Soviet rival and set about working with Ciba and Hoffman to bring anabolic-androgenic steroids to the u.s. market. According to his own version of events, the ambition was to develop a form of the drug that had minimal and controllable physical side effects. However, the reality seems to directly fit with the competitive instincts of high-performance coaches and athletes and the business acumen of a pharmaceutical giant. The result was Dianabol, a form of metandienone that was first identified in 1955. Dianabol was patented by 1957 and sales began in 1958. It would become one of the most commercially successful anabolic steroids.

The idea behind Dianabol was to provide a safe way of gaining muscular and strength effects in ways similar to testosterone. Ziegler and Hoffman worked alongside some of the leading weightlifters and bodybuilders in the usa. They also supported Olympic athletes in preparation for the 1960 Rome Games. The initial results were mixed: some weightlifters did not enjoy taking Dianabol or see the benefits, and the u.s. team still missed out on success at the Olympics.[26] However, once the product was on the market, interest soon spread beyond the top level of strength sport competitors to the lower levels and to other sports. There was no rule against using these drugs, so there was no deterrent to consumption. Sport-specific anti-doping rules would not cover steroid use until 1976, and Ciba continued selling Dianabol in the usa until the mid-1980s. Thereafter it was regulated by drug and criminal laws in the usa and many European countries, but production of Dianabol continues even in the present. Underground use also persists, as it has a reputation for being a highly effective steroid with minimal side effects.

By the late 1950s entrepreneurs such as Bob Hoffman were making the most of the new opportunities associated with fitness cultures: hosting large-scale strength events and selling gym memberships, magazines and nutritional products. Strength athletes would learn how to manage their normal diet to suit their training regime, but they were also encouraged to buy specialist dietary supplements to help their muscle development. Hoffman and Ziegler introduced Dianabol to a group of high-profile weightlifters in the run up to the 1960 Rome Olympics. This drug was perceived as an extension of the need for additional protein synthesis that occurs more effectively when using testosterone. Anabolic steroids mimic that effect, ideally without the excessive androgenic impacts of injecting testosterone.

Ziegler was working with Winthrop Pharmaceuticals to find a better form of steroid by the early 1960s. The holy grail they sought was one that improved performance but had no side effects. Between 1960 and 1962 Ziegler supported Louis Riecke, a leading weightlifter from New Orleans who had been the junior national champion in 1955. A combination of the Winthrop pills and Dianabol, along with cutting-edge training methods, produced good results. Under Zeigler's tutelage, he broke the world snatch record in 1964 but missed out on the Olympics due to injury. Another strength athlete working with Ziegler was Bill March, who won five world championships between 1961 and 1965, set a world record for press-ups and achieved top five places in international competitions.[27] While in later years he would express some remorse at encouraging the steroid use that some athletes took to extremes, in 1965 Ziegler said his aim was to achieve 'physical performances now considered SUPERHUMAN!'[28]

Steroid use had spread widely by the 1964 Olympics. The British coach Tom McNab was surprised by what he saw at those Games:

I was there as an observer with my old friend, the late Ron Pickering, and Ron came back with me one day to the hotel at which we were staying, telling me that the American team were taking various pills at breakfast time, vitamins and some new thing called anabolic steroids which they were taking at breakfast. But I'd never heard of such things and it meant very little to me but progressively over the next six years it became clear that body-building drugs were being taken, as there were some pretty substantial changes in performance, particularly in the throws and decathlon.[29]

The rapid spread of steroids from this period onwards was in direct conflict with Olympic idealism, creating a dilemma for those working in sports. For the next fifteen years, there would be no method for detecting steroid use. Even when a test was introduced in 1975 it was almost immediately ineffective, as everyone involved quickly figured out how to avoid getting caught. Steroid use became an epidemic, an industry and an open secret. It soon spread from the niche sector of strength sports into team sports, track and field and swimming. No organization had yet banned these drugs: the ioc and others were waiting for tests to be developed. So the only reason not to use them was simply that of health, although the full health consequences were not yet understood. The ethical approach to steroid use, certainly in some quarters, was pragmatic: they are available, other athletes are using them, if we don't use them we're at a disadvantage, so we need to use them. Success and rewards would come to those countries who followed that logic and devised the best plans for training and drug use, all the while ignoring potential health issues.

There are many examples of steroid use among athletes from the 1960s through the 1970s. British strength athletes were reportedly starting to use them, as 'several' had supported their training for the 1966 Commonwealth Games with a regimen of steroid use.[30] They became common in u.s. college and professional sport. One American football coach told a journalist in 1968: 'I'd say anybody who has graduated from college to professional football in the last four years has used them.' A newspaper investigation in 1969 revealed that top professional teams used them, including the San Diego Chargers, Kansas City Chiefs, Atlanta Falcons and Cleveland Browns. The journalist also noted: 'So widespread is the faith in hormones that there are verified incidents where pro scouts have supplied the drug to college draftees and college recruiters have given it to high school players.'[31]

Similar comments were soon being made about Olympians. Tom Waddell competed in the 1968 Games as a decathlete and later became a doctor. He observed that over a third of the u.s. track and field team were using steroids during the pre-Games altitude training camp. Of the Games themselves, British doctor A. H. Payne said:

> I am sure that one of the factors involved in the magnificent performances was that the use of steroids had by then become widespread. It was rumoured that athletes in all [track] events up to and including the 1,500 metres in the American team were given steroids by their coaches.[32]

By the end of the 1960s a highly organized doping system had emerged in East Germany, although it seems very likely that many of their rivals were also doping. The small country of around 16 million people was created in the aftermath of the Second World War and the reorganization of Europe during the Cold War. Initially still competing as a unified German team, the new country was first represented in the Olympics in 1968. That was a modest showing, as East German athletes won 25 medals in the Summer Games and five in the Winter Games. Around that time research had been conducted on a new anabolic steroid called Oral Turinabol.

Oral Turinabol is now closely linked with East German sport during this time. It was soon manufactured by the state pharmaceutical company Jenapharm. In a highly organized system, this drug was distributed to elite athletes with the support of their coaches and doctors. By 1972 the success was obvious, as their athletes won 66 medals in the Summer Games and fourteen in the Winter Games. They were bucking one of the established patterns in Olympic sport – that medal success is related to population size and GDP. The most prolific medal-winning countries were typically the largest and wealthiest. East Germany had found a focused, efficient and highly effective method of winning medals. One of the key focal points of this system was women's sport. The other unique aspect of the East German system was the detailed accounts kept of the doping doses and outcomes, many of which were taken out of the country and stored in archives in the USA after the fall of the Berlin Wall in 1989. As a result, we have some important pieces of evidence showing exactly how central Oral Turinabol was to East Germany's sport success.

Female athletes demonstrated the success of the organized system. Kornelia Ender was just thirteen years old in 1972 when she won three silver medals in swimming. Four years later she became the first female athlete to win four gold medals at a single Olympics, all of which broke world records. Through the course of her career she would break 32 world records in individual events. She was recognized as East German Sportswoman of the Year each year from 1973 until 1976.

The 1976 Summer Games further showed the success of a scientific approach to talent development and the use of steroids. Recovered East German records indicated that athletes who reached the elite level in their sport would be put on the 'u-m' programme, which meant that their coach and doctor would support the use of doping. There was careful monitoring of the doses, initially only to optimize their impact aligned with training schedules and performance objectives (that is, a medal at the Olympics or World Championships). However, when steroid testing was developed in 1975 and introduced at the 1976 Games, the monitoring came to include a strategy for avoiding detection. It was established that Oral Turinabol 'washed out' of the athlete's body within three weeks, so doses were timed accordingly. Athletes were pre-tested before leaving the country. An excuse would be made for an athlete not to travel to a competition if they tested positive.

Considering its population size and that it was not economically powerful, the achievements of East Germany's elite sport system were remarkable. They finished second in the medal table at the 1976 Summer Olympics, which was dominated by the USSR, who won 125 medals compared to East Germany's 90 and the USA's 94. East Germany was placed second in the table rankings due to their gold-medal haul – the USSR won 49, East Germany 40 and the USA 34. West Germany, which was bigger and economically much more powerful than its eastern counterpart, was well behind in fourth place with only ten golds. It is also of note that East Germany had comparably fewer competitors in the event. They sent 267 athletes, compared with the USSR's 410 and the USA's 396. Clearly East Germany was punching above its weight in international sports. In the same year the country also came second overall in the Winter Olympics, once again behind the USSR and above the USA.

Doping in sport changed dramatically between the 1960s and '70s. This occurred alongside other important sport developments: new coaching and novel training methods; more full-time athletes; improved training facilities and equipment; scientific research into optimizing training and event performances; the new role of sports psychology. Within this context, we can broadly say that between the mid-1960s and the mid-1970s anabolic steroids were, for some groups of athletes, simply another weapon in the armoury for success. They were not banned and there was no testing. The only deterrent was a vaguely defined threat that steroids might lead to some unwanted side effects ranging from heart and organ damage to acne, hirsutism and changes to genitalia.

We have few accounts of athletes admitting outright to using steroids. This could be partly due to the competitive nature of the sports world: no one wanted to give away their trade secrets to rivals. It may also be explained by the stigma associated with drugs as artificial performance enhancers. Even though steroid use was not banned, it was still frowned upon by the media and sports organization leaders, especially those with a tradition of amateurism.

Various sources relate tales of steroid use in the Olympics from 1964 onwards. Harold Connolly was an American hammer thrower and shot putter who had won gold at the 1956 Olympics and started using steroids for the 1964 Olympics, continuing through to 1972. He held the world record for the hammer throw between 1956 and

American shot putter Harold Connolly, pictured here in 1964 with his wife, Olga Connolly (née Fikotova), who won the discus gold medal in the 1956 Olympics representing Czechoslovakia.

1965, increasing the distance from 68.54 metres to 71.26 metres. Thereafter, the world record jumped dramatically: the next holder was Hungarian Gyula Zsivótzky, who threw 73.74 metres just three months after Connolly's record. Within just two decades, athletes from East and West Germany and the Soviet Union had increased the distance to 86.74 metres. Of course, it is impossible to determine the exact role played by steroids in this history of sporting achievement, but it is very likely that many of the leading throwers used them. Despite Connolly's continued steroid use, he only came eighth in 1960 and sixth in 1964, and failed to qualify for both the 1968 and 1972 Olympics.

An American weightlifter who did openly discuss his use of steroids was Ken Patera. During his preparation for the 1972 Olympics, Patera told a newspaper reporter that the difference between him and his Soviet arch-rival was how much they could spend on steroids. Patera did not compete at that event, but in later years expressed his surprise that no official had contacted him after his highly public comments about steroid use.[33] After his weightlifting career Patera became a leading star of the then-WWF – World Wrestling Federation – where he performed alongside such celebrities as Hulk Hogan. He would also later admit that steroid use was part of WWF culture through the 1980s and '90s.

Sport Mirrors Life

There was a clear period of time when the use of pharmaceuticals grew quickly in society and then, as a natural by-product, in sport. This marked change occurred in the years following the Second World War. For around fifteen years, drug use in sport developed without any restrictions. Amphetamines and related drugs became increasingly common across sports and anabolic steroids were slowly becoming used and accepted by strength athletes. Although amateur sports organizations were the first to articulate concerns about the use of artificial performance-enhancing substances, stimulant use appeared to be just as common in elite amateur and sub-elite sport as it was among the professionals. There was evidently demand, and a new industry of supply. The explanation for this lies in a web of cultural and policy changes that bled into sport from broader society.

The sociologist Nikolas Rose argued that by the mid-twentieth century Western societies had shifted away from religious ideals and divine cures. These societies increasingly sought chemical solutions to psychiatric problems. Amphetamines worked on the central nervous system to reduce fatigue and improve alertness and mood. People began to imagine that new drugs could help them battle depression, anxiety and similar ailments. Rose called this the 'neurochemical self' and explained that pharmaceutical companies marketed products not just as cures for clear ailments but as ways to enhance capacities in already well individuals. As a result, these drugs became normal for day-to-day lifestyle purposes rather than just for treating specific illnesses.[34] For both the recreational and the serious athlete, being competitive was becoming part of their lifestyle and reflected their sense of self, ambitions and reputation. It made sense, then, to try legal and not unhealthy ways to support that competitiveness.

Alongside these drug industry changes were sports industry changes. In a period of peace and prosperity leisure-time activities became a larger part of Western economies. The Olympics were a prime example of this expansion of sports commercialism. The 'Austerity Games' were held in London in 1948 with just over 4,000 athletes from 59 countries. After the relative successes of the Games in 1952 (Helsinki) and 1956 (Melbourne), the 1960 Games in Rome were a larger event, with 5,300 athletes from 83 countries. A similar growth occurred in the Commonwealth Games, which had 590 athletes from twelve countries in 1950, increasing to 860 athletes from 35 countries by 1962.

As competitive sports grew and intensified, so did the support structure. The British Association of Sports Medicine was founded in 1952, the *British Journal of Sports Medicine* was launched in 1964 and the American College of Sports Medicine was founded in 1954. As previously noted, the four-minute-mile barrier fell and opened the door to new possibilities for athletes. In team sports such as football, the status of successful players was growing along with opportunities for sponsorship deals. Public interest in sport combined with commercialization to create more avenues for career enhancement.

For some athletes the normalization of pharmaceuticals in wider society correlated with their own ambitions by making the use of drugs not just acceptable but perfectly logical. Given how slow the sports organizations were to introduce any form of prohibition, it is hardly surprising that athletes undertook doping regimens. Indeed, it is more surprising that big pharmaceutical companies were not upfront about the potential value of their products for athletes, and that team managers were not better organized in planning doping programmes.

Beginning the Struggle for the Meaning of Sport

Before we explore the origins of policy and testing, it is worth considering why doping did not become a fully integrated part of sport in the 1950s. What held athletes back from using drugs? The explanation lies, at least in part, in the essence of sport – put more prosaically, what people think sport is for and about. Ideas about sport have varied across time and place. For some competitors and their coaches, the only thing that mattered was winning. At its extreme, this idea leads to excessive risks being taken in order to achieve victories on the field of play. A commonly cited, though dubious, survey from the 1980s is alleged to have discovered that a high proportion of Olympic athletes would have sacrificed their long-term health for the sake of a gold medal. However, many athletes from the 1950s and even to the present day are committed to sport as part of a culture that promotes good health, friendly rivalry and the ethics of self-discipline, perseverance and fair play. Roger Bannister is an example of this. He did not indulge in the stimulant use that other athletes did in the 1950s. For athletes like these, the use of drugs undermines the reason why they are attracted to sports as a hobby or career.

Anti-doping ideology and policy since the 1960s has been underpinned by a sense that the motivations to use drugs relate to external forces that need to be controlled: excessive individualism, national prestige and politics, financial reward and forced doping by individuals, institutions or governments. Thus anti-doping was never just about the taking of pills or injecting of liquids; it was about the *meaning* of that drug use. This meaning was unique to sport, which is why some drugs were legal outside of sport but prohibited for athletes. As we will see, one of the ambiguous prohibitions is that of blood doping, as it does not involve a drug but is a procedure often involving the athlete's own blood, which can hardly be deemed a narcotic or a criminal substance.

It is hard to imagine, but the period between the end of the Second World War and the early 1960s was something of a golden era for amphetamine use. They were produced by global pharmaceutical companies, sold all over the world and advertised as cures for all manner of both innocuous and fairly serious physical and mental health ailments for all social groups, young and old. They were associated with extra 'pep', a sense of elation and excitement, energy and verve. They were praised by members of the military, workers in industry, artists and writers alike. It is no wonder they ended up being used by athletes.

As we will discuss in the next chapter, critical incidents relating to amphetamine use galvanized anti-drug sentiment in sport from the late 1950s onwards. Several voices would begin to echo the comments of sports doctors that 'something must be done' to stop athletes across sports from risking their health by overdosing these drugs.

From the perspective of twenty-first-century ideas about clean sport and regulated anti-doping environments, it is controversial to say that athletes who used amphetamines in this era were not doing anything wrong. But as we have shown, athletes were simply taking a day-to-day stimulant that was used by millions. This was in no way what doping would become (partly as a result of anti-doping efforts): an underground, secretive means of finding drugs and other techniques that were at the cutting edge of science. Rather, amphetamine use in the 1940s and '50s might best be understood as similar to caffeine use: socially accepted, easily accessible and harmless in moderation. The post-war doping crisis is only a crisis when viewed through the lens of subsequent events.

3

The Beginnings of Testing

Even as amphetamine use was reaching its apex in many countries, anxieties about the impact of doping increased through the 1950s both within and outside of sport. Indeed, concern over stimulants even reached the Vatican. In 1956 Pope Pius XII had said that he was concerned about these 'gravely noxious substances', a comment eagerly picked up by the IOC and repeated in its bulletin.[1] In February 1960 the president of the IOC, Avery Brundage, raised the issue with IOC members with a vague suggestion that some response was required.[2]

Stimulant use continued unabated in cycling at the end of the 1950s and into the 1960s. As we will return to later in this chapter, the legendary French cyclist Jacques Anquetil was open about drug use in the 1960s. He was the first to win the Tour de France five times, doing so first in 1957 and then consecutively from 1961 to 1964. Anquetil was the best cyclist of his generation. He also had a career that began and then peaked while amphetamine use was acceptable but was then brought to an end when new anti-doping rules started to take effect.

One event in the 1960 Rome Olympics brought doping into sharper focus: the death of 21-year-old Danish cyclist Knud Enemark Jensen during a 175-kilometre race. Amphetamines were quickly blamed as the cause of his death. However, Jensen's tragic demise has been consistently misinterpreted since the early 1960s, for two main reasons: first, the collision of the two worlds of elite cycling and amateur Olympics; second, linking this death with amphetamine use helped anti-doping campaigners' arguments for regulations, testing and bans for those who were caught. However, as is often the case with simplistic assertions about the harms of doping, the truth is more nuanced.

Jensen was part of a strong Danish team, but he started having problems during the race. He veered off the road and had to be held up by two of his teammates. When he eventually fell off his bike, the medical staff took him to a hospital tent, where he sadly died. In the days following Jensen's death, the Danish team manager said he had given the riders a drug called Roniacol, a vasodilator designed to improve blood flow. There was no evidence that Jensen actually used amphetamines, but the story soon grew into a 'doping death' scenario anyway. In fact, the conditions of the day were partly to blame. The race took place in the high heat of the afternoon on a 40°C (104°F) summer day in Italy. The hospital tent was even hotter, possibly approaching 50°C. The probable explanation is that Jensen died of heatstroke and culpability should have fallen on the event organizers for not taking care of the competitors. Instead, the blame shifted to the team manager and to the young cyclist, whose legacy remained tarnished until Danish media investigators in the early 2000s found the original autopsy report, which said no drugs were found in his body. Despite a police investigation at the time, no action was taken to pursue a criminal case. However, the story circulated in newspapers, was supported by medical experts and was often referred to by writers seeking to support anti-doping in the ensuing decades. Even the World Anti-Doping Agency had a short history of doping on its website in which it was claimed that Jensen had died from amphetamines, until the information was removed in 2017.

It is ironic that in the same year that the American weightlifting team was using Dianabol, all the anti-doping criticism was

Sir Arthur Porritt (centre), the first president of the IOC Medical Commission from 1961 until 1967.

focused on Jensen. Nonetheless, his death provoked a reaction within the IOC hierarchy. Brundage instructed Sir Arthur Porritt to set up a medical commission that would include the development of anti-doping rules. Porritt was the quintessential upper-class amateur. He represented New Zealand in the 1924 Paris Olympics, coming third in the famous race with Harold Abrahams that was depicted in the film *Chariots of Fire*.

This move by the IOC president to set up a committee charged with organizing anti-doping was really the first international example of the institutionalization of anti-doping. It would also go on to shape how anti-doping shifted from a nebulous concept to a highly impactful policy. Other international sport organizations also discussed ways to control doping in their conferences and internal committee meetings and in partnership with research scientists. This is the period that made anti-doping what it is today by crystallizing various strands of regulation and morality, at the heart of which was the notion that all athletes should be 'clean'. This approach was premised on two ideas: that science would provide the methods of control, and that legally binding policies would provide sufficient punishments to deter prospective dopers. These developments raise intriguing questions about the history of sport: how and why did sport move from the wide use of stimulants without much criticism to athletes becoming subject to stringent drugs rules, intense private scrutiny and the extremes of public humiliation and career-ending stigma?

The Italian Origins of Testing

The first localized anti-doping surveys and testing took place in Italy, headed by Antonio Venerando. They began in 1955 with a research project under the remit of the national sports medicine federation, Federazione Medico-Sportiva Italiana (FMSI), where Venerando was president from 1961 until 1970. His team conducted tests on 'a few sporadic analytical capsules confiscated from athletes, all of which proved to have a basis of beta-phenylisopropylamine'.[3] This means they found Benzedrine. A follow-up study involved taking 25 urine samples from cyclists just after a race. Of these, five contained Benzedrine.

The FMSI and the Italian cycling federation hosted the first ever dedicated anti-doping conference in 1955 amid concerns about cyclists' physical and mental health risks associated with amphetamine use. Writing in 1964, Venerando highlighted two specific cases. The first was that of a cyclist who was admitted to a psychiatric hospital in 1956 due to 'his mind being deranged as a result of excessive recourse to amphetamine products'. The second was two years later and involved another cyclist who admitted to using drugs and was banned from sport for life after he went into shock during a race 'induced by excessive recourse to sympathetico-mimetic drugs'.[4]

The Italian group met during the 1960 Olympics under the title of the International Conference on Psychoergopharmacology, though we do not have any historical records from that meeting. The following year the FMSI partnered with the Italian Football Federation to assess the extent to which players were using stimulants. The survey results showed that 17 per cent were using 'amine substances'. From there, the Italian group held two meetings in Florence in 1962 that included leading pharmacology experts, such as the pharmacologist Daniel Bovet, who had won the Nobel Prize in Medicine in 1957.

These initiatives were a few years ahead of the IOC, who are largely credited with leading anti-doping. It was the Italians, however, who created a model for anti-doping that would pre-empt those established by larger and better-resourced organizations. They were the unrecognized pioneers in the field. The FMSI drew up a convention for anti-doping work in football, and a campaign focusing on football teams from July 1962 to June 1963 appeared to have some effect: a survey of players in 1963 found prevalence of just over 1 per cent. By coincidence, it was during this time that the English press uncovered the purple hearts scandal involving Everton players.

Testing also began in Italian cycling and the results from one amateur race showed that more than half the cyclists had taken Benzedrine. The principle behind this anti-doping work was to reduce health risks by using educational programmes and testing. There is no sign that these programmes contained underlying moral justifications relating to 'clean' sport found within the Olympic and amateur sport circles.

The Anti-Doping Laboratory of the Sporting Medicine Centre in Florence was created by the FMSI for analysing samples. Positive results were reported to the relevant sports federation that would decide on punishments. The FMSI was also aware that a formal definition of doping was required and produced one in 1962:

Doping is to be defined as the absorption of a substance intended to increase artificially the performance of the subject while participating in a sporting event, this being incompatible with the ethics of competition and with physical and mental integrity. The following preliminary list of prohibited substances is given to supplement this definition: (1) amphetamine and its derivatives; (2) substances similar in action to amphetamine; (3) anti-MAO; (4) caffeines. It should be pointed out that these substances are not only the most commonly used, but can be easily detected.[5]

Venerando attended the first major international conference on drugs in sport, held by the Council of Europe in 1963. He told them that he believed 'the situation seems ripe for an early and permanent solution to the doping problem on a European scale or even world-wide scale.'[6] This might seem optimistic now, but it is worth remembering that the use of stimulants appeared to be a manageable problem – they had a short-term effect and were detectable in urine samples taken just before or just after competitions.

If we closely examine the FMSI's definition we can see that, far from providing a solution, international scientists and sports leaders were embarking on a challenging course of action that would sow the seeds for decades of flawed, failed and disproportionate anti-doping policy-making. Central to all definitions of doping in the 1960s – many of which were probably influenced by this one – is the idea of natural versus artificial. The first international definition was agreed at the 1963 Council of Europe meeting and stated that doping was 'the administration, by any means, to an individual in good health of a substance foreign to the body or of abnormal quantities of physiological substances, with the sole aim of artificially and unfairly enhancing individual performance in a competition'.[7] The idea of 'artificial' is both vague and highly problematic. In a broad sense, much of sports performance is artificial: tailored diet and nutrition plans; equipment, which can range from basic shoes and uniforms to specialist gear like that for the pole vault; mental and psychological training techniques; coaching and skill development. The athlete is manufactured, not natural; made, not born. Even if we focus just on diet, the challenge for anti-doping was and remains how to draw a clear and distinct line between what is acceptable and what is not. Why, for example, has it always been acceptable to consume any number of supplemental vitamins and any amount of protein, or to use paracetamol to relieve pain? These could all be categorized as 'artificial' and aimed at enhancing performance.

The second part of the Italian definition is also vague and hard to implement. How could it be judged whether or not a specific substance increased performance? In theory, there would have to be a controlled study of athletes both with and without the potential doping substance to assess if performance was enhanced. But there are many factors that can impact an athlete's performance on a specific occasion, including their health, emotions and the weather. Indeed, numerous studies (in different sports and countries) have proven that teams playing at home have a 'home advantage', which presumably would also count as artificial and unfair on the away team. Sport is not a level playing field.

The list of substances to be prohibited is intriguing. Amphetamines are understandable, given what was known about their benefits. Substances 'similar in action' is vague, as it does not specify which actions or effects. The term 'anti-MAO' is confusing, as monoamine oxidase inhibitors, more commonly known as MAOIs, are a class of drugs used to treat depression and would have a stimulant effect. Caffeines is pluralized, which is strange, but caffeine is a stimulant that can enhance performance. It was banned in some sports through the twentieth century, but in the early 2000s the world of sport finally decided not to bother. Indeed, the very idea that several cups of coffee might lead to a ban from sport now seems preposterous.

Overall, one key point missing is threshold levels: would any amount of these drugs, no matter how small, lead to punishment for doping? If so, would all punishments be equal, or would there be gradations? Another general point is that the sole focus is on use at the time of competition and there is no indication that athletes would face regulation of stimulant use at any other time. As would become apparent in subsequent years, even the definition of 'participating in an event' is not that straightforward and would require a specific timeframe indicating when an athlete becomes subject to in-competition anti-doping rules. Would, for example, an hour before a race be classified as part of the event? If that is too long, then what is reasonable? Thirty minutes? Ten minutes? Without realizing it, and probably unaware of the looming steroid crisis, the architects of anti-doping in the early 1960s were putting a policy in place based on a vague idea, and it would require highly complex scientific, legal and bureaucratic machinery to make it work. A generous interpretation is that they could not foresee the problems on the horizon. A less generous view is that they over-simplified the issues in the search for solutions and messages about 'clean' sport. They were idealists.

Morals and Evil

When the Council of Europe arranged the 1963 conference, the idea was to collate ideas from various organizations, including the IOC, that were beginning to see doping as a problem for sport. Two meetings were held that brought together representatives from fourteen countries including Austria, Belgium, France, Italy, the Netherlands, Spain, Switzerland, Sweden, Turkey and the UK. These discussions would help focus international efforts, as the Council of Europe itself could not direct policy.

The official report was full of grave warnings: 'Drug-taking and other methods of stimulation by athletes have implications going beyond the sphere of sport: medical, moral, legal, social and commercial.'[8] Doping was considered to be a 'social evil' presenting a hidden danger that the public was largely unaware of. These are clearly signs of an emerging moral panic – an exaggerated response to a relatively minor issue viewed as a threat to moral values – and an attempt to promote reactions based on imaginary scenarios of doom and gloom. The report noted:

> All participants attach great importance to European co-operation in stamping out the doping of athletes, which they regard as a social evil having ramifications far beyond the realm of sport . . . Experience shows that in those sports in which doping is already prevalent, the moral and physical consequences of the practice have already begun to undermine the whole structure of the sport. If doping is allowed to grow unchecked, the time will come when all the benefits accruing to the individual and to the community from the practice of sport will be lost.[9]

The handful of specialists at these meetings had a strong sense of mission. The Council saw itself as setting the course of action for the rest of the world to follow. One of the participants was the Austrian doctor Ludwig Prokop, who would play a significant role in anti-doping during the following decades. His contribution to the conference included the claim that concerted efforts to promote anti-doping 'should result in effective protection against the immoral act of doping. Thus we shall be able to continue to keep the ideal of sports pure, for the welfare of all mankind.'[10] The authors of the report noted, 'Apathy on the part of those morally responsible is a crime against humanity.'[11]

It is hard not to notice an undercurrent of self-appointed leadership, collective egotism and an almost fundamentalist fervour. The language of good and evil was infused throughout these early policy meetings and reports. The final section of the report is entitled 'Fighting an Evil'. Venerando himself outlined the moral threat of doping and the necessity of finding solutions:

> Doping, like any other form of drug addiction or contagious disease, cannot be eradicated in one country alone; it must be fought steadily, with equal pertinacity and determination, in all other countries as well. In Europe at least, and more particularly among the nations of common Latin origin, the anti-doping campaign should be given practical form as rapidly as possible, and be translated from words into action. The Italian experience can be of great value here, facilitating the immediate practical results which are needed to avoid the risk of further damage and unethical victories won by fraud. Young people will then return to sport with unblemished aims, competing by fair means and restoring to sport its primary function as a means of preparation for life itself.[12]

There were some important leading figures who collaborated in this enterprise and who overlapped with other organizations' efforts. Antonio Venerando's colleague in FMSI, Giuseppe La Cava, was contacted by the IOC in February 1962 to help them determine what did and did not constitute doping and which actions could be taken.[13] Three months later, La Cava set forth his position on doping for the IOC's *Bulletin*. He focused on amphetamines as drugs that produce such a stimulant effect that any competition results would not be a true reflection of the athlete's ability and endeavour. He therefore saw those drugs as 'illegitimate from the point of view of ethics' and medically dangerous because they mask the natural signals and sensations of fatigue.[14]

It is one of the overlooked aspects of the history of anti-doping that a small group of Italians laid the foundations for how doping

Avery Brundage, president of the IOC, 1952–72; photographed here in 1964.

would be defined and controlled, although they quickly found themselves at the same table as many others who felt a sense of purpose in supporting anti-doping efforts, all of which aligned with the increasingly anxious media coverage of specific cases. Their efforts were subsumed and overshadowed by the IOC, which integrated anti-doping into its 'Olympism' ideology.

The IOC was the first international sports organization to formally respond to this issue, with its leadership apparently united on the principles of anti-doping. President Avery Brundage requested action, and so the Medical Commission was created in 1961. An important feature of the IOC's policy creation and development was that doping control was defined as a scientific issue, to be led by scientists, but with a foundational rationale that referred to fairness, integrity and morality. As the criminologist Kathryn Henne noted, this early approach set up a tension between technologies. On one side were 'bad' technologies, which allowed athletes' bodies to be manipulated; on the other were the 'good' technologies deployed by anti-doping scientists to regulate such manipulations.[15]

This is perhaps best captured in the report presented to the IOC at its meeting in Moscow in June 1962 by the medical experts J. Ferreira Santos and Mario de Carvalho Pini. The report was also summarized for the international sports community in the IOC *Bulletin*. In it, the focus was again on amphetamines and related drugs. The pair called on the IOC 'to take adequate measures in this combat against doping, a practice which is the very symbol of the negation of the ethics of sport. This practice is growing every day and its ill-effects are felt by the human race.' We see here a broadening of the issue. This moved doping away from being the simple act of taking a stimulant pill that was common in many parts of the world (and indeed had bolstered war efforts only two decades previously), and towards it being a crisis for humanity as a whole. Santos and Pini wanted a full-scale educational campaign addressing the harmful effects of doping, which they saw as going beyond just health risks. They characterized anti-doping as a fight against evil:

> At the present time, sport is affected by a real menace and evil: the practice of doping. It prevails in professional as well as in amateur sport. This evil must be fought. Doping provokes a false feeling of well-being which may lead the athlete to a state of auto-intoxication resulting from the physical effort he has made. It may also cause a physiological intoxication through the taking of a drug having damaging effects on the life and health of the athlete. Drugs capable of increasing the physical and mental output of the athlete artificially should certainly be prohibited.[16]

The anxieties around doping were gaining momentum. This growing unease can be traced primarily to the early work in Italy, the reaction to Jensen's death and the interest taken by the Council of Europe, the IOC and other sports organizations. The pivotal years were 1957–68: from the early research and first conference on the subject in Italy to the first international testing in the mid-1960s and the first Olympic rules being implemented in 1968. The prominent influencers were men with both a medical background and some previous involvement in sport, often as amateur athletes.

A prime example was Arthur Porritt, chair of the Medical Commission from 1961 to 1967. He oversaw the establishment of a testing system and the first List of Banned Substances for the Olympics, produced in 1967 and implemented at the 1968 Summer and Winter Games. Born in 1900, Porritt became the house surgeon at St Mary's Hospital in London in 1926 and was appointed personal surgeon to the future King Edward VIII. His bronze medal at the 1924 Olympics was followed by additional sporting achievements as he went on to captain the 1928 New Zealand Olympic team and was their team manager at the 1934 British Empire Games and 1936 Olympics.

After a highly decorated military career, Porritt returned to London to resume his medical career. He resumed his duties with the Royal Family, acting as surgeon to George VI and Elizabeth II. He had joined the IOC to represent New Zealand in 1934 and continued in that role until 1967. At the time that he was given the task of setting up the Medical Commission he was also president of the British Medical Association and of the Royal College of Surgeons. In other words, the man entrusted to tackle the issue of doping was coming at it not only from a medical perspective, but with decades of experience of amateur and Olympic sport, for which doping was an ideological wrong. It is perhaps no surprise that he wrote in 1965: 'Doping is an evil – it is morally wrong, physically dangerous, socially degenerate and legally indefensible.'[17]

The idea of doping as evil, immoral and corrupt had taken root among a coterie of sports doctors and leaders who began to see this as an issue that needed attention. Porritt was far from alone in his assessment. A number of other medical experts with an interest in sport were expressing their concerns. In 1963 the assistant secretary of the British Association of Sports Medicine, J.G.P. Williams, wrote that doping

> is a form of moral deception in which the athlete is achieving his results not on his own merits, but artificially, and in a manner contrary to the code of sportsmanship – in short he is cheating, and persistent cheating may be the first step in the downward path to moral degradation, especially if he gets away with it.[18]

Williams would contribute a great deal to the research literature on sports medicine. In 1963 he became a Fellow of the Royal College of Surgeons and was awarded the Gold Medal from the International Federation of Sports Medicine in 1980. While his contribution to elite society was not as marked as Arthur Porritt's, he was – like many other anti-doping campaigners – a member of well-established organizations in and out of sport.

It is noteworthy that the language used to vilify athletes who used amphetamines was not the same as the language used to criticize other amphetamine users. Those who overdosed with the drug were seen as pathological and self-destructive; those who used it for creative and artistic purposes were seen as degenerate and anarchic (although their creative outputs were celebrated); those who used it for recreational purposes were equated with junkies. The drug itself had many uses, but it had very specific connotations in sport – cheating, the masking of fatigue, an artificial method. This was not a simple spillover from wider society. Rather, this was the invention of anti-doping: a unique way of defining and managing drug use, with its very own way of dealing with – and demonizing – (ab)users.

Rules and Testing Take Shape

The first set of experimental tests for amphetamines at international multi-sport events were conducted at the 1964 Olympics in Tokyo. The impact of public concern was expressed in January 1964 by the IOC Member for Sweden, Bo Ekelund, who was 'disconcerted by numerous press reports of doping cases' and called for the introduction of blood tests to detect offenders. A scientific meeting was held to discuss doping during the Games that was attended by individuals already involved in other organizations, such as Albert Dirix, Williams and Prokop, who acted as chair. The definition of doping presented at the meeting echoed those of the Italian group and the Council of Europe:

> Doping is the administration to, or the use by, a competing athlete of an agent foreign to the organism by whatsoever route introduced, or of physiological substances in abnormal quantities or introduced by an abnormal route, with the sole intention of increasing artificially and in an unfair manner the performance of that subject.[19]

There was a certain ambivalence to the IOC's approach to doping. While they had appointed Porritt to lead the charge, they had also declined the invitation to join the Council of Europe meetings on the basis that this was a sport problem and should be left to sport organizations. While they allowed some indicative testing at the 1964 Games, Porritt's report in the aftermath was met with some resistance. The leadership refused to endorse his requests for a declaration supporting anti-doping, of sanctions for any National Olympic Committee (NOC) or individuals who promoted drug use, that NOCs should make athletes available at any time for testing and that athletes sign a declaration that they did not use drugs and were willing to be tested.[20]

There are a few potential explanations for this veto. One is that Avery Brundage himself did not really see doping as a major issue. For him it was a subset of the broader and more serious threat posed by professionalism. Doping seemed isolated at this stage to 'pep pills' and to specific sports like cycling, athletics and football. Professionalism, however, threatened the very foundations of Olympism and the meaning of the Olympic Games. Brundage also had a pragmatic view that the IOC did not have the power to impose anti-doping rules, or the financial resources for testing, so the responsibility should lie with the international sports federations. After all, the Olympics were only held once every four years and athletes competing at the event were not under the IOC's jurisdiction at any other time. The IOC was not yet the financial success it would become – ironically, after giving way to professionalism in the late 1970s and the media-led commercialism of the 1980s. Instead, the 1950s and '60s were an austere period in which they relied on volunteers and the host nation's ability to pay for facilities. As such, if doping was to be addressed then the individual sports federations themselves should pay for it.

Nonetheless, the IOC was happy to allow Prokop, Pierre Dumas and Dirix to initiate the first ever testing programme at an Olympic Games in 1964. Dumas was the official doctor to the Tour de France and had undertaken some inquiries into cyclists' use of amphetamines during the 1962–3 season. In 1962 he approached the Union Cycliste Internationale (UCI), the international governing body for the sport, to ask for their support. The UCI's reply was passive, declaring that there was nothing that could be done to prevent cyclists using drugs.[21] But Prokop, Dumas and Dirix were at the forefront of raising this issue. For example, Prokop attended a race in Austria where he 'found the sweatshirts of a number of

Austrian cyclists padded with large quantities of amphetamines and other stimulants'.[22]

In light of the rumours surrounding Knud Enemark Jensen's death, a variety of accidents and medical crises among professional cyclists, and the ways key sports doctors moved between cycling and the Olympics, it is little surprise that the 1964 testing focused on cycling. We might also speculate that cyclists were viewed with some suspicion by the Olympic old guard, as there was a long tradition of professionalism and underhanded tactics in that sport. The testing in Tokyo involved three forms of control: a search for evidence that drugs had been injected before a race started; a search of cyclists' equipment and clothing at the starting line; and collecting urine samples for analysis. Potentially undermining the effort, the cyclists had been told of these investigations before the event and there were no formal rules preventing doping. It was likely very unclear to everyone involved what might actually constitute a doping offence. However, there were no positive tests from the urine samples.

Despite the efforts of these pioneers, there was a degree of scepticism within the broader sport community that the methods for testing were sufficiently accurate and many saw that more research was required. Arnold Beckett, a research pharmacologist from Chelsea College, London, had been working with colleagues on developing a test for amphetamines and related metabolites since the late 1950s. Beckett would become one of the leading anti-doping scientists in subsequent years, but his initial introduction to the field seems to have been largely accidental.

Along with his departmental colleagues, he presented a paper in March 1965 at a conference held at Chelsea College – the International Research Symposium on Medical Chemistry. He was approached by a Belgian scientist, Paul Janssen, who was in the audience. It is not clear if Janssen had a formal role within sport but he was a hugely successful and respected scientist until his death in 2003. Janssen explained to Beckett that the challenges facing sport organizations' attempts at testing for amphetamines related to timing and reliability. Beckett would later reflect that the testing conducted at the 1964 Games used a technique that was not sensitive enough. He also said that it was Janssen's idea to take the Chelsea group's new research to the IOC and others in sport.

Within a short period of time, Beckett's more refined methods were introduced at a major event: cycling's Tour of Britain in 1965. Over the fourteen-day race, the testers worked hard and almost all the riders were tested at some point. Some were even tested more than once. Beckett's method returned the results in less than 48 hours. This led to the first ever doping scandal underpinned by scientific testing procedures. The race leader, the Spaniard Luis Pedro Santamarina, was caught doping. He was disqualified along with two of his teammates and an English competitor, Ken Hill. The reaction from the Spanish team was such that the race organizer, Harry Merrell, said at the time: 'It came as a terrible shock when we got the news that four riders had had positive tests. We thought at one time we were going to have a riot on our hands.' The story was front-page news in the British press.[23]

The football World Cup was the next major sporting event to be subject to testing procedures. Again, we cannot say for sure what the rules were or what the players had been told about drug use, even for medical purposes. The fact that the 1966 World Cup was being held in England and that it was English researchers who were leading the way on testing was a twist of fate that offered an opportunity. Football's governing body, FIFA, was not demanding immediate action on the issue of doping and none of the leading anti-doping doctors of the day were closely associated with football. However, there was some evidence from the Italian testing that footballers were using amphetamines, and of course the Everton scandal had happened only three years earlier.

No players tested positive at the World Cup, or at least not positive enough to justify a punishment. Beckett wrote after the event that his team found 'very small amounts in urine and it was established subsequently that these had arisen from the use of certain nasal drops by some competitors'.[24] There are several issues to note here. First, the players were using a nasal spray, presumably to help their breathing, that contained amphetamines or a related substance. This shows how normal these drugs were at the time. It also shows how hard it was (and would become) to distinguish between medical use and performance-enhancing use of prohibited substances. Second, it is far from clear what information and education the players had received. Had they been told not to use any substance that might be banned or that those substances could be in products like nasal sprays? Finally, did players take the opportunity to deliberately dope and then invent a story about innocent medical use when caught? These ambiguities were evident even at these earliest days of testing, and they would become much more of a problem as doping became widespread through the 1970s and '80s.

In fairness to the 1966 testers, they did organize the sample collection method and set up protocols to ensure anonymity. They also introduced an independent verification system so that the samples were not tampered with and were analysed correctly. This system would underpin future anti-doping methods.

The ioc had decided in 1967 where the focus of its efforts would lie and planned to introduce testing at the 1968 Winter and Summer Games. In May of that year Arthur Porritt presented his report. The Medical Commission was then re-organized with the Belgian aristocrat Prince Alexandre de Merode appointed as chair, a position he would retain until 2002. The definition of doping accepted at this time was not dissimilar to that first outlined in the late 1950s in Florence: 'the use of substances or techniques in any form or quantity alien or unnatural to the body with the exclusive

Prince Alexandre de Merode (left), chairman of the ioc Medical
Commission, 1967–2000; pictured here in 1971.

aim of obtaining an artificial or unfair increase in performance in
competition'.[25]

The Commission also published a detailed 'List of Banned
Substances', a project led by Porritt and supported by a report written by Martyn Lucking, a British doctor and former shot putter.
The report claimed that these drugs had been used in sport 'since
at least 1963', an oddly precise but inaccurate time point. The identified substances were 'Alcohol, Amphetamines and Ephedrine,
Cocaine, Vasodilators, Opiates, Cannabis'. They went on to make
a tentative reference to steroids, cautious of the fact that there was
no scientific analysis available for detection: 'the use of Anabolic
Steroids (except for medical purposes) constitutes "doping" from
an Olympic viewpoint.'[26] This was accepted by the ioc Executive
Board to be implemented at the next Games.

The list of banned substances was strange given that the rationale for anti-doping was largely the widespread use of stimulants.
While it might be good for athletes' health and the safety of others,

including spectators, to stop athletes – especially in shooting, javelin, archery and such like – from having impaired judgement caused by alcohol, it is far from clear how and why alcohol was put on the list. Almost all the pre-1967 justifications for anti-doping focused on artificially trying to improve performance. Alcohol has the opposite effect, apart from in situations such as what apparently occurred in 1968, when a nervous young man about to compete at shooting had a couple of beers to calm down. A member of the Swedish pentathlon team, Hans-Gunnar Liljenwall, was found to have 'too great an amount of alcohol in their system', leading to the whole team being disqualified. Three medals were subsequently returned by the Swedes to the IOC. Liljenwall thus has a place in history as the first ever Olympian sanctioned for doping. The limit set by the IOC appears to have been 0.4 parts per thousand.[27] He would also be the only person to receive a doping ban for alcohol consumption at the Olympics, even though alcohol remained on the banned list until 2018.

Response to Early Anti-Doping

While much of the doping debate focused on cycling, there were conflicting attitudes towards testing. As noted, the 1965 detection of doping in the Tour of Britain prompted anger rather than support for anti-doping. Similarly, when testing was introduced at the Tour de France in 1966, the cyclists protested by staging a 'go slow' and voiced their dismay at this intrusion into their professional identity and culture. The world's leading cyclist, Frenchman Jacques Anquetil, went public with honest statements about the use of stimulants. He claimed that all riders doped and that races would be slower and less exciting without drugs. Anquetil was a colourful character who enjoyed socializing and drinking. He was also widely adored by sports fans, winning the French sportsman of the year award in 1964. He famously broke the world hour record

Jacques Anquetil, Tour de France, 1962.

in 1966, but had his record annulled after he refused to provide a urine sample. French president Charles de Gaulle said of Anquetil in 1994: 'Doping? What doping? Did he or did he not make them play the Marseillaise abroad?'

Anquetil's openness about doping, and indeed cycling's liberal attitude towards testing, did not last long. In the summer of 1967 on the gruelling Mont Ventoux stage of the Tour de France, the Englishman Tommy Simpson fell off his bike and was rushed to hospital, where he died. The publicity around Simpson's death was international and included evidence that he had taken amphetamines. Like Jensen's, Simpson's death was likely brought on by other factors. It was a very hot day and riders were allowed only two bottles of water, so he was probably dehydrated. There was also a lack of on-site medical support. He had drunk some brandy, since knowledge about the dehydrating effects of alcohol had not yet been established. Despite this, Simpson has been associated with a turning point in the history of anti-doping ever since – a stark, highly visible symbol of the risks associated with the use of stimulant drugs in sport.

The contexts for doping were wide and varied. The IOC could only focus on its quadrennial event, frequently asking for help from the international federations to take responsibility for education and testing. The IOC was worried about the costs involved (in fact, the cost of hosting the event itself was troubling enough). Steroids were also beginning to spread among elite athletes, some of whom competed at the 1968 Games. Cycling was slowly introducing testing, but drug use had become widespread and nearly an inevitable part of a cyclist's career. Simpson told a journalist in 1960:

> I am up there with the stars, but then suddenly they will go away from me. I know from the way they ride the next day that they are taking dope. I don't want to have to take it – I have too much respect for my body – but if I don't win a big event soon, I shall have to start taking it.[28]

Amphetamines were found in his jersey on the day he died and the post-mortem found traces of amphetamines and alcohol in his system. Other teammates also provided anecdotal evidence of his drug use. Simpson was something of a pioneer as one of the first British professional cyclists to join a European team. A memorial stone in his honour remains on Mont Ventoux. Yet in the same year top Belgian cyclist Rik Van Steenbergen gave a frank account of why the very nature of professional cycling lends itself to the inevitability of doping:

I've had to drive to Paris, then immediately after the race get back in my car for a 10-hour trip to Stuttgart where I had to get on my bike at once. There was nothing to do. An organizer would want this star or that one on the bill. He would pay for it. Another would want the same ones the next day, and the public wanted something for its money. As a result, the stars had to look fresh in every race, and they couldn't do that without stimulants. There are no supermen. Doping is necessary in cycling.[29]

The 1960s was the decade of revolution in one sense, as drug-testing rules and procedures were established and implemented in some sports. The ideas and methods would continue to underpin anti-doping even in the present day. There was a strange mixture of idealism, pragmatism and failure. The idealism would foster a culture of intolerance, leading some athletes to be punished for minor offences, much like Hans-Gunnar Liljenwall in 1968. At the 1972 Games, sixteen-year-old swimmer Rick DeMont lost a gold medal and the chance to win other events when he tested positive for ephedrine found in his asthma inhaler. He had declared this to the u.s. Olympic Committee, but they had not received an agreement from the IOC to allow it. The pragmatic policy, certainly within the IOC, was to ignore steroids until they had a test in place, which would take until 1975. And the failure was evident: doping simply could not be controlled. There was not enough funding for testing, there was no mechanism for out-of-competition testing and it was easy to beat the tests by timing consumption and excretion rates.

The role of the IOC's Medical Commission is key to understanding the initial approach to anti-doping and how regulations would unfold in subsequent decades. These early tests and policy developments worked to centre science in the sport doping narrative. Athletes who were willing to improve their performances but corrupt their natural abilities with 'artificial' substances were cast as the villains, while the scientists and medical researchers working to prevent them from doing so were seen as heroes. Science-based anti-doping was deployed to uncover immorality by detecting physical evidence of doping. This 'good' scientific approach would always be flawed, though. Testing technologies have been chasing doping technologies in a perpetual game of catch-up since the first tests by the Italian researchers in the mid-1950s.

The most significant flaw, however, was that anti-doping only addressed the symptoms of doping, rather than the underlying causes rooted in the pressures faced by athletes in highly competitive environments. Anti-doping was based on the idea that sport was not that serious – athletes could and should be amateurs and role models for fair play and good health. But increasing professionalism and nationalism would soon make the quest for any and all performance-enhancing measures seem a normal part of sport.

4

How Doping Became
an Epidemic

High-profile scandals during the 1970s and '80s made it clear that many athletes were using steroids, but the historical development of their use is an under-appreciated part of sports history. Androgenic-anabolic steroids, to give them their full name, completely changed the nature of elite sport, including the Olympics, and transformed bodybuilding and gym cultures. Bodybuilders pushed the very concept of human limitations by reshaping the human form, sometimes in extreme ways. These kinds of body alterations prompted anxieties around technology, progress and transhumanism. The focus of this chapter is on sports rather than general fitness. But similarly to those who used amphetamines, steroid-using high-performance athletes were reflecting a wider cultural pattern that was unregulated and widespread. Once again, however, athletes were treated differently by policy organizations and regulators. The rules on steroid use in sport were more stringent than outside of sport and testing was frequent.

Anabolic steroids are a synthetic form of the hormone testosterone. 'Anabolic' refers to the muscle-building capacity of the drugs; 'androgenic' means male sex characteristics. The key distinction in the way stimulants and steroids are used by athletes is that the latter are used throughout training programmes, but most would stop using them before competitions. Conversely, stimulants are most effective during competition. This difference forced anti-doping testing to change course since it would no longer be sufficient to obtain samples during competition. Anti-doping authorities would need to find ways of accessing athletes at times when they would likely use steroids. Doping, and therefore testing, moved into their homes, training centres and even their holidays. The definition of doping had to change as well to include new classes of substances. Anti-doping also introduced complex rules on threshold levels. The science of testing required increased sophistication and sensitivity, and the number of laboratories that could run the tests needed to expand dramatically. The cost of running such a complex and rapidly expanding system would quickly become a problem for sport.

Steroid use and the response to it was also gendered. Female athletes building their muscles were sometimes criticized both within and outside of sport as they challenged the perceived norms of female physicality. This history is also linked to the introduction of sex testing in the 1960s. Some national governments actively promoted steroid use in their bids to gain national sport prestige. The obvious and highly detailed example is that of East Germany, though other countries in the Cold War 'Big Arms Race' had similar, if less aggressive, approaches. It is widely assumed that the Soviet Union had a system like East Germany's but we lack the historical documentation to say that unequivocally. Western countries allowed smaller groups to collectively dope, and for sport organizations to avoid testing athletes too rigorously. Gender and politics came together in East Germany as the national leadership saw women's sport as a great opportunity to win more medals. They did not shy away from giving female athletes anabolic drugs, ultimately leading to one of the most shameful episodes in the history of sport as girls as young as twelve years old were forced to take steroids. This was often done without consent, or even without their knowledge or the awareness of their parents or families.

GDR swimmer Kornelia Ender, 1973. During her career, she broke 32 world records and won four Olympic golds, eight World Championship golds and four European Championship golds.

It is estimated that 10,000 athletes were given steroids in East Germany between the mid-1960s and the late 1980s.

This chapter will focus on the period from the early 1970s to the mid-1980s. As noted earlier, athletes were experimenting with these drugs around the time of the 1968 Olympics, if not earlier. They were widely used by the 1972 Games, but mainly in strength sports. Steroid testing was introduced in 1975. During the late 1970s there was innovation in the production and supply of steroids, offering users a much wider range of products. By the 1980 and 1984 Olympic Games steroid use was an uncontrollable epidemic threatening the very essence and existence of the Olympic movement. By this time, their use had spread into professional team sports.

Medical and scientific advice also changed over this period, from initial scepticism that the drugs would enhance performance to the promotion of a fear-based health message. This message centred on warnings that steroids could have a whole host of physical and psychological side effects, and could even prove fatal. Meanwhile, the supply side was expanding to meet the demands of these new consumers. Simultaneously, detailed knowledge and understanding of both optimal use and excretion rates to avoid testing positive were also improving. In these ways, steroids impinged on idealized notions of health and fair play, were an 'open secret' in elite sport for at least two decades, and became an uncontrollable crisis for sport organizations when they led to several scandals in the late 1980s and '90s. These cases and the negative attention they afforded the IOC and other sport organizations eventually led to a global response in the form of the World Anti-Doping Agency.

Beginning a Losing Battle

In the years preceding the 1972 Olympics, the IOC published a short pamphlet for athletes informing them of anti-doping rules and procedures. Anti-doping rules were formalized in the Eligibility Code. This stipulated that athletes should be amateurs, observe the traditions and ethics of the Games, and not use drugs or artificial stimulants of any kind. The only way to enforce this last clause was through testing, but the cost of such testing provoked some concerns. Setting up a laboratory just for the event was priced at $1.5 million (this is around $9 million in today's money, but the IOC was not a wealthy organization in the 1970s). Athletes were tested at the 1972 Games, but there was, of course, no test for steroids yet. Still, testers were kept busy at the Games by 2,078 urine samples and 65 blood tests that led to seven disqualifications.[1]

Awareness of steroid use was growing. East German sports leaders made the decision to implement a programme of organized doping because they believed many (or most) high-level athletes in competing countries were already using steroids.[2] By 1972 British coaches and reporters had also identified this trend. In *The Guardian*, John Williams wrote:

> For some years now it has been known that certain athletes in the power events have taken these body building drugs in enormous doses in combination with very heavy weight training programmes and high protein diets. The results are in the record books for all to see.[3]

The British Olympic weightlifting coach John Lear was brutally honest about his concerns that steroid use was so widespread:

> How does one deal with a sport in which cheating is so prevalent that it is no longer considered cheating? My future role as a coach at international level has already been described as that of a 'needle man'. It is a role I will continue to reject.[4]

The issue was openly addressed in a BBC *Panorama* documentary in 1972. Much of the focus was on the emerging UK bodybuilding culture, which was highly influenced by what young British athletes saw was happening in the USA. However, it also included an early reference to the spread of steroid use from strength sports into track and field. One of the interviewees was the UK national athletics coach, Wilf Paish. He told viewers that athletes were looking for the steroids they thought other countries' athletes were using:

> I'm in an awkward situation but I don't condemn them at all. It's difficult for me to condone them in my position

but I certainly don't condemn them because I feel athletics is wanting to be the best, the best in the world. And it's very difficult to be the best in the world these days unless you're on steroids because I'm fairly certain the standards set throughout the world are influenced by athletes who have or still do take this drug . . . I feel now it's gone so far that we can't beat them, we're almost going to have to join them.[5]

During the Games in Munich an unofficial survey was conducted by the American athlete Jay Silvester, who was then the world record holder for discus. Silvester competed in four Olympics (1964–76), with his best result being a silver medal in 1972. He broke the world record four times, twice in 1961 and twice in 1968 – the last stood until it was equalled in 1975. He asked around a hundred athletes, mainly from strength sports, if they had used steroids. The answers came from a wide geographical range: the USA, the USSR, Egypt, New Zealand, Canada, Morocco and Britain. Apparently, 68 per cent admitted to using them.[6]

In the aftermath, Silvester told a reporter: 'All the throwers and weightlifters and "heavies" of any ability in these Olympics have taken or do take anabolic steroids . . . if you don't take steroids you are bound to be handicapped in the heavy events.'[7] He also drew an important comparison between Western athletes who had to take steroids on their own, and 'Eastern bloc' countries where users received state medical support. There is some evidence that the Western style of individual, semi-informed and uncontrolled doping created risks that the supervised East German athletes did not face (at least the older athletes, who knew what the pills they were taking contained).[8] Widespread use is unsurprising given that there were no regulations to stop athletes from doing so. This was also the phase of use best defined as 'early adoption', before the health scares, media-fuelled moral panic and scandals that

Jay Silvester, who asked Olympic athletes about their steroid use in 1972, pictured here in 1970.

would plague later decades. It was a period of relative innocence surrounded by a sense of optimistic potential.

Another American athlete in the same Games, Ken Patera, explained in an interview not only that he used steroids but that the difference between him and his arch-rival, Russian Vasily Alexeev, would be the extent of their respective usage:

> Last year, the only difference between me and him was that I couldn't afford his pharmacy bill. Now I can. When I hit Munich next year, I'll weigh in about 340, maybe 350 [pounds]. Then we'll see which are better – his steroids or mine.[9]

Patera was not coy about his extensive use or the fact that he intended to improve his performance through steroids, as he made clear to the American media. When he was later asked about the controversial nature of this statement, Patera replied that he 'didn't hear a peep out of anyone from the u.s. Olympic Committee'.[10]

Several Canadian athletes and coaches shared Patera's view on the necessity of steroids to compete internationally. Bruce Pirnie, a Canadian shot putter who competed in both the 1972 and 1976 Olympics, used steroids in his Games preparation. He was first introduced to them while attending college in the usa and then cycled their use for nearly a decade. Pirnie later changed his stance to be vocally anti-drugs when he became a collegiate coach, but recognized that the steroid-fuelled records of his competitive era were unlikely to be broken without their aid.[11] Many other Canadian athletes and coaches were also discovering the perform-ance benefits of steroids in the early 1970s, which would lead to widespread doping among some of the country's best known ath-letes. Canadian sprinter and Ben Johnson's future coach Charlie

Ken Patera (left), u.s. weightlifter.

Lord Killanin, president of the IOC, 1972–80, pictured with
Princess Beatrix of the Netherlands, 1976.

Francis reported first becoming aware of the extent of steroids
while competing in the Munich Olympics.[12]

The IOC's response to this emerging trend was delayed by
the lack of scientific testing to detect steroid use. However, Lord
Killanin had taken over as president from Avery Brundage just
after the Munich Games and was determined to prevent doping
from becoming more widespread. He was a hereditary peer, having
taken his place in the House of Lords in 1927 at the age of 21,
succeeding his uncle. In 1950 he took the role of president of the
Olympic Council of Ireland, then became his country's representative at the IOC in 1952 and was elevated to vice president in 1968.

In 1973 Killanin addressed doping in a speech, bringing it to
the forefront of policy issues: 'I believe that doping is a subject as
serious as the whole question of eligibility [of professionals] and
the size of the Games.'[13] In his own 1983 biographical account,
he reflected that doping was for him 'the most obnoxious aspect
of sport' and that such cheating would lead 'to the destruction

of competition as we know it'. Moreover, he thought steroid use reflected what earlier anti-doping enthusiasts had focused on – the line between natural and artificial:

> The Olympic ideal is to create the complete person – not an artificial one. Unfortunately, through commercialization and politicization, this ideal is being subverted and, through the efforts of certain doctors, the body is being more and more tampered with to its own detriment.[14]

It is hard to tell if he was thinking here of male or female bodies, or both. Men were getting larger and stronger; some women had broader shoulders, larger and more defined muscles, deeper voices and additional hair growth. Sex testing had been introduced in the late 1960s and critical observers focused on these changes to female athletes' physicality. In 1976, when the East German swimming team were accused of having deep voices, their coach reportedly replied: 'We have come here to swim, not sing.'[15]

Developing a Test

The years between the 1972 and 1976 Olympics were crucial for the introduction of a test for steroid use. Avery Brundage had encouraged the ioc Medical Commission to start investigating options in 1971. Prince Alexandre de Merode knew of the research conducted by Arnold Beckett into amphetamines but this had not yet shifted to steroids. This might have been a reason (though it is uncertain) why the uk Sports Council awarded a research grant in 1972 to F.T.G. Prunty of St Thomas' Hospital in London to find a method of detecting steroid use.[16]

Prunty's research does not seem to have directly influenced the next stage of scientific development. Beckett approached Raymond Brooks, who worked in the same hospital as Prunty, but apparently the two scientists did not collaborate. Instead, Brooks and other researchers developed their own new techniques. An antisera 'with the desired specificity for certain characteristic features of various types of anabolic steroids' was presented in a paper by N. A. Sumner in 1974. Brooks and his colleagues then published a paper outlining radioimmunoassay methods, which were highly sensitive in 1975. Meanwhile, Ward and colleagues used a gas chromatographic mass spectrometric method for finding a parent drug and its metabolites in urine after the positive result was produced by the radioimmunoassay method.[17] These were highly important developments in anti-doping scientific knowledge, the first steps in preventing rampant steroid use, even though only a handful of laboratories in the world had the necessary equipment to run such tests. Similar to a decade earlier, the work of a select group of scientists – doing this work as a sideline to their main professional ambitions and responsibilities – would change the nature of sports performance and ethics.

An experimental run-through of these initial methods was undertaken at the 1974 Commonwealth Games in New Zealand. Of the 55 urine samples in the trial, nine failed the radioimmunoassay method test, and seven were confirmed positive using the gas chromatographic mass spectrometric method.[18] We do not know if the athletes were given prior warning about the testing. However, seven out of 55 is a relatively high return, especially considering that none of the major superpower countries attend the Commonwealth Games. There was no USA, West Germany, East Germany, USSR or any of the Eastern bloc countries, where prevalence has always been assumed to be higher. These trials at the Games were held in February 1974 and testing was successful enough that it took only two months for the IOC to add anabolic steroids to its list of banned substances.[19]

This new testing approach was announced ahead of the 1976 Olympics in Montreal. The IOC was working with the IAAF in developing the protocols and procedures, though some experts sat on the relevant committees for both organizations. The IAAF Medical Advisory Panel was first formed in 1972 and included Arnold Beckett and Ludwig Prokop, among others. Ironically, it also included Manfred Höppner, who by that stage had become a leading figure in the East German doping programme. Other key European scientists were supporting this effort: the German Manfred Donike, whose Cologne laboratory would play a central role in anti-doping, and the Swede Arne Ljungqvist, who would also become another longer-term proponent of anti-doping science and policy. The IAAF trialled a steroid test at the 1974 European Championships in Rome but was uncertain about the accuracy of its testing processes. One of the central issues, and a barrier to rapid progress, was the complex equipment required. In the mid-1970s only three laboratories could run both types of tests and two more could run one type.[20]

Along with the costs and practicalities of testing, another issue was that most major sports medicine organizations were taking the position that steroids did not actually improve strength or endurance. It would not be until the early 1980s that the ACSM would admit that steroids were powerful contributors to bodybuilding and competitive sports. Around that same time, various clinical and populist publications would critically highlight the side effects and warn users of their dangers.

The group of IAAF and IOC scientific experts predicted the explosive growth of steroid use and tried to pre-empt potential harms to users and to the image of sport. Steroids played neatly into the framework already established for anti-doping: they artificially enhanced performance, they were a form of cheating and they had health risks. However, moral certitude gave those in charge of pioneering anti-doping a certain smug satisfaction – they were on the side of good. This small band of doctors and pharmacologists were changing the world of sport, in their eyes for the better. If athletes cheated, they should face the consequences. Who could argue with that? These pioneers based their self-regard on the idealized belief that sport could be drug-free and the imagined sense that authorities had the power to catch users. Yet, unknowingly, they had set in motion what would become one of the biggest ongoing failures in the history of sport, a failure that would also lead to unintended harms as the 'war on doping' evolved and was empowered to reach more athletes for increasingly innocuous violations.

The 1976 Olympics testing served only to prove that doping was going on undeterred by the new anti-doping efforts. Only eight athletes were caught for steroids; the other users were wise enough to know that a carefully managed 'wash-out' period would be enough to avoid a positive test. The athletes were from Sweden and Czechoslovakia, with two apiece from the USA, Poland and Bulgaria. All were male weightlifters apart from female Polish discus thrower Danuta Rosani. It is surprising that these athletes did not plan their wash-out period properly, given how well known this practice was among athletes. One of the Bulgarians was Blagoy Blagoev, who lost a silver medal after testing positive and being disqualified. He was hugely successful nationally and internationally, setting 23 world records, winning silver at the 1980 Olympics, silver at two World Championships (1979 and 1980), gold at three European Championships (1979, 1981 and 1982) and three consecutive World Championships golds (1981–3).[21] We do not know if he used steroids throughout his career, but given their widespread use and the consistency of his success, there are obviously grounds to suspect it.

We know that the East German doping programme was ramped up in 1974 with a formal policy called State Plan 14.25. In 1976 East Germany came second in the Winter Olympics medal count, well behind the USSR but clearly ahead of the USA. They were also second in the Summer Olympics, although this was a bit closer. The USSR were first with 125 medals (49 gold, 41 silver, 35 bronze), but East Germany still managed 90 medals (40 gold, 25 silver, 25 bronze). Although the USA won more medals overall, they were positioned third owing to having won fewer golds, with 94 medals overall (34 gold, 35 silver, 25 bronze).

Anti-doping scientists at the front of testing technology were not fooled by the low numbers of positive tests and knew that more athletes had successfully doped without being caught. Indeed, Arnold Beckett was fully aware of the limitations of the steroid test, writing in the *Olympic Review* (the official magazine of the IOC) in 1976:

> A competitor may take anabolic steroids during training, then discontinue their use two to three weeks before a particular event; a urine sample collected at the event may not show a positive result even though the competitor may still be having an advantage at least in weight from the drug misuse.[22]

There was a broad sense that steroids were necessary in many Olympic events and in professional team sports. The genie was out of the bottle. To be sure, the Eastern bloc was not a unified entity when it came to sport or doping. Individual countries kept secrets from each other and East German government officials were as keen to demonstrate they were not simply a Soviet puppet state as they were to beat the Yankee capitalists.[23] The organization of doping from the highest levels of government is unlikely to have occurred only in East Germany. Many have speculated that such a system also existed in the USSR, though as mentioned we lack evidence for that claim. In North America and Europe the response was ambivalent and diverse. There were sections of the sporting community who pushed forward an anti-doping agenda through education, moralizing statements and scientific research. Governments and sports leaders accepted that the public expected 'clean sport' and so ostensibly supported anti-doping endeavours.

Life was more complex behind the scenes, as shown by the authors of a 1977 U.S. Presidential Commission report. At the heart of their analysis was the notion, and related anxieties, that communist countries were ahead of the USA, both in terms of Olympic success and in their understanding and use of steroids. The remit of the report was to explore why the USA's performances in the Olympics were declining in comparison with other countries. Much of the focus was on how sport was organized at school and university levels. However, there were some open and honest discussions about steroid use. First, there was a feeling that knowledge about steroids was limited and while there were potential side effects these would likely be reversed after usage stopped. This was more or less exactly what the East German leaders thought at this time. The broad context was summarized as:

> At present, tremendous controversy surrounds the use of anabolic steroids by athletes. A great deal of research is being done throughout the world to examine the impact of these drugs on performance. However, the studies are not well-controlled, results are not well known, and the effects of these substances on the human body are not fully understood.

In addressing the comparative situation, the authors wrote that in the USA: 'Very little of this information [on doping] is properly disseminated to the [U.S.] sports community . . . In failing to recognize the importance of medical research to athletic programs,' it argued, the USA 'lags behind other nations, such as Canada and East Germany, which have spent millions of dollars to coordinate their reference programs and research in human performance'.[24]

It is noteworthy that they refer to Canada here, as one of the famous aspects of the 1976 Olympics was that it was the first time a host country had not won a gold medal. Canadian athletes and coaches were beginning to develop a network of steroid use, advice and supply by 1976. The shot and discus thrower Bishop Dolegiewicz competed at the 1976 and 1984 Summer Olympics and became known as an information and supply source for athletes looking to take up a steroid programme. Famously, he was the person responsible for initially providing steroids in the early 1980s to former Canadian sprinter turned athletics coach Charlie Francis, who would gain global infamy in 1988 as the coach of Ben Johnson.[25] Though he was aware of steroid use from his competitive days, Francis began to realize how far into the sprint events use had gone when he was told by a Canadian athlete that the Canadian's British 100-metre runner wife (the couple were likely Brian Saunders and Andrea Lynch) was on a steroid regimen in 1979. Francis was also becoming aware of widespread use in the USA, leading to fears that his athletes were actually falling behind the Americans.[26]

The report authors interviewed one of the American weight-lifters who tested positive at the 1976 Olympics (his name is not given in the report). He was naturally disappointed at being disqualified, but shifted the focus to the lack of support given to American athletes and his feeling of being isolated and left to make his own decisions. The authors note:

> the drug disqualification can be viewed as the fault of our system. Medically and politically naïve, American lifters are characterized by a leading medical expert as not knowing 'which pills to take, how many to take, how long to stay on them or how long to stay off them'.

The report continued and took a position that was not that of the IOC's anti-doping, clean sport stance. Instead, it was a realistic assessment of the situation:

many athletes have been taking [anabolic steroids] in an effort to improve their performance . . . many weightlifters say they know of no champion lifters who have not taken steroids at some time in their lives. The Eastern Europeans in particular are known to have taken large doses of the various kinds of steroids as a regular part of their supervised training programs, without suffering disqualification in competition. Escalation in the steroid race makes many American athletes feel compelled to take steroids in order to be able to compete effectively . . . athletes who receive informed guidance in the use of these drugs continue to perform exceedingly well in international competition, and most u.s. athletes are forced to fend for themselves.[27]

We do not know whether these comments had a direct impact on sports policy. There is no evidence that the USA set in motion an organized approach to doping, although it did set up new training centres to focus on Olympic success. There is, however, plenty of evidence that subcultures of steroid use blossomed in various parts of the country and in a wide range of sports.

Within the span of just a few years the whole pharmacology of steroid use changed, the black market grew rapidly and use was an open secret in high-level sports. However, the biggest anti-doping 'catch' of the late 1970s was in the 1978 football World Cup. Scotland player Willie Johnston was sent home after testing positive for the stimulant fencamfamine, which was included in an over-the-counter medicine he had taken for hay fever. Given what had happened to Rick DeMont in 1972, it should have been obvious to critical observers that a policy designed to stop systematic cheating was not only failing to meet that lofty ambition, but was leading to punishments for accidental use.

After the 1979 invasion of Afghanistan by Soviet forces, the 1980 Moscow Olympics were the focus of political arguments.

A total of 66 countries boycotted the Games, including the USA. Some countries, like the UK, sent smaller contingents. With fewer countries represented, the medal table was dominated by the USSR with 80 gold, 69 silver and 46 bronze. East Germany came second with 47 gold, 37 silver and 42 bronze, while Bulgaria was a distant third with 8 gold, 16 silver and 17 bronze. In spite of the boycott, and the recently introduced test for steroids, 36 world records, 39 European records and 74 Olympic records were set at these Games.

The doping situation was well managed to avoid detection by this point. East Germany, and possibly the USSR, tested its athletes before they left the country for international competitions. The on-off cycle of steroid dosages was well understood by many athletes and their support staff. Even so, the fact that no athletes tested positive during the 1980 Olympics remains highly suspicious, especially given that the USSR and East Germany were so dominant. Quite how much of an organized conspiracy existed to avoid any positives remains an ongoing question. The British investigative journalist Andrew Jennings reported that a KGB colonel later admitted that anti-doping efforts at the Games were thwarted by KGB officers posing as IOC officials (a tactic that was repeated at the 2014 Sochi Winter Olympics). This apparently led to many Soviet athletes being 'rescued with [these] tremendous efforts'.[28]

In 2016 a Soviet doctor called Grigory Vorobiev, who had been the chief medical officer for the national track and field squad, told the *New York Times* that steroid use was very common:

> By the 1970s, he said, most of the several hundred athletes with whom he worked were asking about performance-enhancing drugs, particularly after traveling to international competitions. When athletes sought advice in individual consultations, he said, he told them to take 'as low a dose as possible,' cautioning them to watch for cramps or changes

in voice as signs that they had overdone it. Most of all, he stressed that drugs were not a substitute for rigorous training. Not everyone chose to use illicit substances, he said, defending Soviet sports as not uniformly tainted. He was unable to estimate how many athletes had used drugs, adding that some who had shown drastic physical changes had denied doping during private consultations with him. But low doses of oral steroids were common among top track athletes, Dr Vorobiev said, asserting that if he had dissuaded them from taking drugs, he would have been blamed for poor results and summarily fired.[29]

He also showed the reporter an official document from 1983 showing that the Soviets wanted to raise the level of steroid use in preparation for the 1984 Olympics, which they ultimately did not attend owing to the political boycott of the Los Angeles Games.

There is also some scientific evidence that many athletes had doped in preparation for the 1980 Games. Although the scientific equipment and procedures followed by the Moscow laboratory were closely observed by the IOC, German anti-doping scientist Manfred Donike had been given permission to check all the samples in the aftermath of the event. Strangely, that permission was granted before the event, as if the IOC expected there could be an issue. Donike applied a new test he had developed for exogenous testosterone levels, setting a generous ratio of 6:1 (testosterone: epitestosterone). He discovered that 20 per cent of the samples were positive, and those included sixteen gold-medal winners. As the sports historian Jörg Krieger observed:

the results prove that the doping control system was by no means as efficient as was widely believed by many anti-doping laboratory experts at the time. Despite their increasing efforts, there remained many loopholes for athletes. The usage of performance-enhancing substances was well-advanced in comparison with the analytical methods.[30]

We do not know which countries the sixteen gold medallists came from, although the vast majority of golds went to the USSR and East Germany. However, the 20 per cent testosterone positives is likely just the tip of the iceberg, as many other athletes would have used steroids and ensured they washed out of their system in time for the tests. The Soviets gave the impression of taking anti-doping seriously, and the only indication that they deliberately corrupted the process is the above anecdote from Andrew Jennings. However, we could speculate that their detailed knowledge of how the testing would be conducted allowed them to carefully manage the doses and excretion rates ahead of the event.

The unavoidable conclusion about the broader context, however, is that anti-doping policy and testing was a complete failure. It was impossible to prevent steroid use without a fully comprehensive system in which athletes were tested frequently throughout the year, not just during competitions. The competitive nature of sport had a snowball effect on doping behaviours. If an athlete and their coach imagined that their closest rivals were doping, then they believed they had no choice but to try and keep up. The Pan-American Games in 1983 showed the world that doping was not confined to communist countries.

The Pan-Ams were held in Caracas, Venezuela. A total of 36 nations competed, with the USA, Cuba and Canada topping the medals table. Testing for steroids was announced just before the event started, leading to fourteen disqualifications. Of these, eleven were in weightlifting and included athletes from several countries: three from Cuba, two from Canada and one each from the USA, Venezuela, Argentina, Puerto Rico, Chile and Nicaragua. The others were in cycling (Chile) and athletics (Dominican Republic). Further, it was reported that twelve U.S. track and field athletes withdrew from the event when they heard that testing was being conducted. The success of the anti-doping effort was in part due to the introduction of new methods developed by Donike to detect synthetic testosterone.[31] However, it seems that the organization of doping and communication of how to manage doses and excretion was not well advanced, as was suggested in the 1977 Presidential Commission report. Being able to avoid detection was as important as any part of the doping process.

One of those disqualified was Canadian weightlifting champion Guy Greavette, who had won two gold medals and a silver. In the aftermath, he spoke candidly and publicly about the steroid culture in sport. He told the Canadian Broadcasting Corporation:

> I started to take steroids in 1980 . . . and then in 1981 I started to take it more regular; I don't take very much of them, I take them for short periods of time . . . I understand there are some risks . . . I'm sure that there are probably some bad side effects, if you abuse a drug, I don't feel I have abused it; I've used it, but I haven't abused it.[32]

His coach, Aldo Roy, was equally unrepentant: 'As coaches, we're all amateurs, we're all volunteers in this organization; as with other organizations, our duty is to expose the athletes to the pros and cons . . . I think you have to educate people.'[33] In contrast to the sense of dramatic crisis that would make all talk of doping taboo in the twenty-first century, Greavette and Roy were refreshingly honest. As the Canadian sports sociologists Ian Ritchie and Greg Jackson explained:

> Greavette expressed his perception of the 'relative' harms from steroids, a far cry from today's anti-doping policies' 'all or nothing' outlook on the dangers of drugs; rarely is room made for a 'middle ground' position, even with respect to

potential health concerns. Finally, coach Roy's suggestion that a coach's job is to 'educate' athletes regarding the 'pros and cons' of potentially using performance enhancers would rarely be made in today's anti-doping climate; few coaches today would admit to giving such 'nuanced' advice to his or her athletes, without facing public condemnation if not formal reprimand.[34]

This was a time when steroid culture expanded internationally. The health risks of use, especially overuse and polydrug use, were suspected but not known. It would be the stories from East German athletes after the fall of the Berlin Wall that raised the level of critical condemnation. Greavette and Roy also had a pragmatic view of steroids. They perceived them as an opportunity to support sports performance and believed that, if managed correctly, this could be done without any meaningful harm to the athlete. They were also indicative of a culture of doping that was emerging in Canada, as we know that many Canadian strength and track and field athletes were doping from the early 1980s onwards. This culture would be fully exposed after the 1988 Ben Johnson scandal. Greavette also competed in the 1988 Olympics. In an interview in 2002, Roy gave the impression that he suspected the weightlifters within his group might be on steroids, but he didn't know for sure: 'We told all the athletes who were there at the training camp, if anyone's on steroids they've got to be off, like months ahead of the event. If you got caught you were stupid.'[35]

Greavette was also interviewed in 2002 and said he had pondered the choice of using steroids for over two years. He came to the conclusion that it was not possible to be a successful weightlifter without them. His teammate, Larry Burke, had the same view: 'I used steroids. I didn't use a lot but I used them. And I don't think I would ever have got to those levels without steroids.'[36]

For all its faults, anti-doping was beginning to have an impact. Testing forced athletes to think carefully about use, dosage and risks. However, the 1983 Pan-Am Games was the first time that steroid use became a scandal as the story was front-page news in the Canadian media – another 'dark side of sport' scandal that supported the simplistic ideas upon which anti-doping was founded and developed.

The stigma associated with being a doper was obvious. Greavette felt 'dropped' by friends, colleagues and sports organizations. He was given a two-year ban, meaning that he missed the 1984 Olympics for which he was a gold-medal contender. In Burke's words, he was 'hung out to dry' by the authorities.[37] In the USA Jeff Michaels suffered similarly. He was stripped of three gold medals from the Pan-Am Games and disqualified from the 1984 Olympics. This was the beginning of the crackdown, the gradual emergence of a draconian view of doping and dopers. There was still no overarching anti-doping policy, punishments were decided on an ad hoc basis and testing was sporadic and limited. However, in the years preceding the 1984 Olympics the tide was starting to turn against steroids.

The Steroid Moral Panic and Its Implications

The ACSM declared in 1977 that steroids had no effect on sports performance. During a conference in 1984 the organization's leaders decided to alter this position and accept that steroids could enhance performance if used alongside a weight-training regime and high-protein diet. In the interim Allan Ryan published two articles (in 1978 and 1981) outlining the pros and cons of steroid use. Ryan was a founding member of the ACSM, and served as its president from 1963 until 1964. This is where we begin to see scientific critique around the questions of performance effect and of whether the health risks are severe enough to justify testing and education interventions:

From 1965 to 1977, 25 clinical studies were published dealing with the administration of an anabolic-androgenic steroid to adult human males for evaluating changes in strength and, in 10 of these studies, in maximum oxygen consumption. In 12 of these studies, improvements were claimed from the use of these steroids; in the other 13 no improvements were observed. Other studies have shown that in healthy adult males these steroids reduce testosterone and gonado-trophin output, which reduces spermatogenesis. Alterations of normal liver function have been found in up to 80% of persons treated with c17-alkylated testosterone derivatives. Peliosis hepatitis, with liver failure and death, and fatal liver cancer have also been reported in adults so treated. Reliable methods for detecting anabolic steroids in the urine are now used in certain international competitions. Testing, announced bans, and disqualifications have not been effective in controlling the use of the drugs. The best hope for doing so lies in continuing education of athletes and their supervisors.[38]

Bob Goldman, Patricia Bush and Ronald Klatz published a book in 1984 called *Death in the Locker Room: Steroids in Sports*, which included an influential critique of steroid use. In it they detailed a series of cases in which overuse or polydrug use had led to severe illness or death. Sections of the media were beginning to take more interest in doping as a scandalous topic. Of course, some previous doping events had been treated in this way, such as the Everton amphetamine story in 1963, though Tommy Simpson and Knud Enemark Jensen were covered in a more balanced way that focused on the tragedy of their deaths rather than blaming them for doping. The coverage of the Pan-Am Games cases, however, framed doping as inherently wrong: it didn't matter how much or little of a substance was taken, whether the athlete won or lost or whether that athlete had or had not suffered any health consequences. Crucially, the focus was placed squarely upon the athlete, and they were defined as a cheat. This form of cheating was invested with a higher level of emotive criticism than other forms of cheating.

Steroid use was expanding through various populations, informed by gurus like Dan Duchaine, who published the *Underground Steroid Handbook* in 1981. Duchaine realized that West Coast America was a hotbed of opportunity. As American journalist and author Shaun Assael explains:

> The Olympics were coming to Los Angeles in 1984 and with them a caravan of athletes who would be on the lookout for the latest muscle-building concoctions... five years after the debut of [the 1977 documentary] *Pumping Iron*, everyone in LA wanted the Schwarzenegger look. More ominously, a new disease that was killing gay men in San Francisco had begun its fatal migration down the Pacific coast. Gay men were turning to steroids to prevent the disease's wasting effect.[39]

Duchaine worked with Mike Zumpano to write a guide to steroid use that covered 29 different drugs, with details of their effects and how to use them. They even suggested to readers where to buy the drugs and gave pricing information. The *Handbook* took Duchaine and Zumpano ten days to put together and they had a friend print copies of the eighteen-page booklet in his garage. They advertised it in the magazine *Muscle Building and Power*, at a price of $6. Within a week they had $500 worth of orders. Soon they had gone global, with 5,000 ordered from France and an additional 3,000 from Germany. Within a couple of months they had sold 80,000 copies, earning them nearly $500,000.[40]

The supply side of the steroid trade was innovative and creative, with sellers supporting users and looking to future customers. The

Canadian thrower and steroid supplier Bishop Dolegiewicz was well known within athletics for his willingness to supply steroids in the 1970s and '80s, as well as for offering advice on how to use them. He would counsel athletes, especially young athletes, on how to properly dose, cycle and minimize side effects. He also aided athletes with practices like injections.[41] This type of knowledge dissemination normalized steroid use throughout sport, leading the steroid black market to grow quickly. Athletes could avoid testing positive easily and there was no out-of-competition testing. On the other side of the fence, anti-doping campaigners and scientists tried to warn users about the health risks, while also trying to improve the testing system. As the Los Angeles Olympics would prove, they were losing the war on doping. They were simply too far behind steroid gurus like Duchaine and Zumpano and they could not control doctors who sold steroids to their 'patients', much less the underground manufacturers and gym dealers. Worse, they did not have the money for adequate testing. Steroid use became an epidemic.

5

The End of Innocence

The 1983 Pan-American Games scandal did not usher in an anti-doping revolution. It may have emboldened the IOC circles that wanted a crackdown on doping and harsh punishments for dopers, including the chemist and test developer Manfred Donike. It may also have made some users cautious about managing their doses and using other avoidance methods. However, by 1983 there were sports doctors in the USA, Canada and the UK, and probably elsewhere, willing to support their clients' demand for performance-enhancing substances. The doping systems of East Germany and the Soviet Union continued apace, but their boycotts of the 1984 Olympics meant that the anti-doping focus at this time fell largely on North Americans and Western Europeans.

On the face of it, the 1984 Games were surprisingly clean. There were only twelve positive tests (eleven were for steroids, the other for ephedrine), with only two medallists disqualified. One was the Swedish wrestler Thomas Johansson, who had won a silver medal. This setback did not prevent him from continuing his career, as he went on to win gold at the World Championships in 1986 and silver at the 1992 Olympics. The other disqualified medallist was the Finnish 10,000-metre runner Martti Vainio, who also had won silver. However, he would later argue that his positive test was the result of accidentally using a steroid he thought was a vitamin supplement. His initial lifetime ban was reduced to eighteen months, after which he returned to competitive racing. The Icelandic discus thrower Vésteinn Hafsteinsson was also disqualified but returned in time for the 1987 World Championships, thereafter competing in three more Olympic Games (1988, 1992, 1996), three more World Championships (1991, 1993, 1995) and two European Championships (1990, 1994). After his retirement he became a coach, including for world and Olympic champion Gerd Kanter. Greek javelin thrower Anna Verouli returned from her disqualification to compete in the 1986 European Championships, two more Olympics (1988 and 1992), two World Championships (1987 and 1991) and the 1990 European Championship.

The lack of internationally organized anti-doping rules meant that punishments were decided on a case-by-case basis. These 1984 cases show that the sports community had not yet demonized doping in the way it would just four years later when Ben Johnson was given a lifetime ban. It may have been related to the fact that no one at the Los Angeles Olympics who tested positive was a high-profile athlete. They were from a wide range of smaller countries: Greece, Iceland, Sweden, Japan, Italy, Austria, Algeria and Lebanon. The legendary American sprinter Edwin Moses, who won gold medals at the 1976 and 1984 Olympics and would later become an anti-doping campaigner, reflected in 2009: 'We knew what was going on [in 1984]. But I don't think it had gotten to the point where it is now . . . the global scepticism.'[1]

Evidence of the wider acceptance of doping that was hidden from public view in 1984 would emerge in due course. One infamous story from those Games is that nine positive doping tests were deliberately destroyed to avoid bad publicity. There are numerous versions of the events. Investigative journalist Shaun Assael explained that the safe where the IOC Medical Commission chairman Prince Alexandre de Merode stored the documents with the test results was removed and taken to a storage facility.[2] The sports historian Thomas Hunt found a letter from 1994 in which the prince claimed that Tony Daly, a member of the Los Angeles organizing committee, had destroyed the records.[3] However, Dick Pound, the Canadian lawyer who would become the first president of the World Anti-Doping Agency in 1999 and was appointed vice-president of the IOC in 1987, put the blame on an organized cover-up involving the presidents of the IOC and the IAAF.[4]

Regardless of which version is true, the IOC leadership has always put a positive spin on anti-doping testing and results. In a way, this was easily done. A small number of positives was used as evidence that pre-emptive deterrence was working, while a larger number of positives was purported to mean that on-site testing was apparently working. The 1983 Pan-Am Games and the ensuing public debates probably led to some doubt that exposing doping fully would be good for the Olympic brand. The 1984 Games is renowned for being a success, ushering in new commercialization methods, including sponsorship from multi-national corporations, and efficient cost management (unlike the Montreal Games, which racked up a debt that would take thirty years to repay). But these accomplishments would certainly have been overshadowed if a high-profile American athlete was caught doping.

The extent of doping around the 1984 Olympics is unknown and evidence is sparse. A California doctor, Robert Kerr, published a book in 1982 titled *The Practical Use of Anabolic Steroids with Athletes*. He was a renowned expert and was consulted by many athletes, and he would later claim to have supplied steroids to around twenty medallists at the 1984 Games.[5] We know that Ben Johnson's steroid programme began around 1981, and he was likely to have been doping ahead of the 1984 Games, where he won two bronze medals. His teammate Angella Taylor-Issajenko worked with Kerr and Johnson's doctor, Jamie Astaphan. Taylor-Issajenko won a silver medal in 1984. At the 1982 Commonwealth Games she had taken home two golds, a silver and a bronze medal.

She would later reflect on steroid use and the stakes of winning
gold medals during this period:

> I always felt people at my level were possibly doing them and
> the people below me wouldn't have beaten me without doing
> them . . . There is a pot of gold at the end of the rainbow.
> It becomes quite tempting. In America, they put you on a
> Wheaties box. The lure of the money is quite amazing. They
> don't even want the silver medalist. You win the Olympics
> and become an instant millionaire.[6]

Other Canadian Olympians had doped in preparation for the
1984 Games. The aftermath of the Pan-American Games failed to
derail the steroid habits of the strength sports contingent. Jacques
Demers won a silver medal in weightlifting, but he would later
admit to having been a regular user of steroids. In what now seems
like a remarkable story, he was caught – along with teammates
Terrence Hadlow, Michel Pietracupa and Mario Parente – smuggling a huge amount of steroids into Canada. They were returning
from the World Weightlifting Championships in Moscow and
were stopped at Montreal's Mirabel airport in October 1983. Their
bags contained 22,515 steroid capsules and 414 vials of testosterone. The Canadian Police force inferred this was a money-making
scheme when the athletes said that one hundred capsules could
be bought in Moscow for \$1 and sold in Canada for \$35. Guy
Greavette told the Canadian media that this was a regular activity: 'It's unfortunate, but nothing new. This has been happening for
years. Those drugs are so much cheaper over there and easier to get,
so you just go for it. You know it's going to help – it's so tempting.'[7]
   Today it seems remarkable that the couriers were not given a
jail sentence for trafficking; nor were they banned from their sport
long enough to prevent Demers competing in the 1984 Olympics.
The Canadian sports authorities were struggling to contain what

was evidently a huge problem. This was becoming an international issue with the growing awareness that Eastern Europe presented an opportunity for buying and using steroids. The Canadian team travelled to that part of the world to participate in competitions and they held annual training camps in Czechoslovakia – all opportunities for athletes to easily access a range of steroids. The East German doping programme was continuing unabated, though it was so highly managed that no non-state-approved drugs were imported or exported.

Doping was also a dirty secret within British sport. During the late 1970s and early 1980s the runners David Jenkins and Drew McMaster turned to doping to boost their performances.[8] Jenkins, to whom we will return, made a successful business of importing steroids with Dan Duchaine. He competed at the 1972, 1976 and 1980 Olympics, while McMaster was at the 1980 Olympics and the 1982 Commonwealth Games. The high jumper Dave Abrahams said those Games were awash with doping: 'On the plane back, most of the English team were talking about drugs. I'd say 80 per cent of them were, or had been on them.'[9]

Internationally renowned British athletes provided additional evidence of doping. In 1986 Tessa Sanderson, the javelin gold medallist at the 1984 Olympics, wrote that 'a year or two ago, a well-known former international thrower said he believed 60 per cent of the British team had at some time used drugs, specifically steroids . . . from my observations I guess he would not be too far out.'[10] Daley Thompson, who won back-to-back gold medals in the decathlon at the 1980 and 1984 Olympics, also estimated that around 80 per cent of Britain's elite athletes doped.[11]

Much as in other countries, the response from sports leaders in Britain was mixed. Some athletes, coaches and officials openly criticized doping. However, the sports sociologist Ivan Waddington has shown that there was an element of complicity and passive support for doping. One example was that testing could be conducted in ways that avoided certain athletes being selected ahead of and during important events – a practice that Charlie Francis also alleged was occurring in Britain. Waddington also highlighted the role of sports doctors and coaches, reporting that British athletes had been provided with steroids by a team doctor who subsequently recorded the effects of the drugs and offered strategies for beating doping tests. Avoiding positive tests was also important, as even highly placed coaches and officials who may have looked the other way with regards to doping would not be able to avoid the scandal associated with a British athlete testing positive.[12]

We cannot verify the involvement of specific individuals, or of how widespread doping was within the highest levels of British sport. It is the case that a number of British sports officials and scientists had led the efforts to stop doping, and continued to do so, within the IOC, IAAF and Council of Europe. At the same time, it seems some of their compatriots were turning a blind eye to doping among athletes. Yet no high-profile British athlete tested positive during the 1980s.

The business of steroid manufacture and supply was booming. The former athlete David Jenkins turned his hand to the supply side after using steroids towards the end of his career. His enterprise involved smuggling steroids into the USA from Mexico. By the mid-1980s he was allegedly responsible for around 70 per cent of the black-market supply. He and 33 others were convicted in 1987 of smuggling more than $100 million worth of the drugs into the country. It was estimated in 1985 that over a million Americans used steroids, with around 40 per cent getting them from qualified doctors like Robert Kerr.[13] That means 60 per cent of users obtained steroids from underground, black-market suppliers and risked all sorts of problems, like cross-contamination, mislabelling, improper dosages and having to rely only on other users' advice. A 1988 report also highlighted the accessibility of doping products to athletes and the general public:

With the more sophisticated forms of drug abuse, there appears to be ready access for any determined athlete, although not by any means on the local shopping basis of anabolic steroids or stimulants. We accept that there is a serious black market in human growth hormone, and there have been well-substantiated incidents of substantial thefts of such material which can only be seen as being planned with the athletes in mind as a market.[14]

Steroid use had spread throughout all sections of sport, with a 1988 survey published in the *Journal of the American Medical Association* reporting that 6.6 per cent of American high-school students admitted using them.[15] Additionally, use of new drugs was becoming common, notably human growth hormone. Much of this information emerged from investigations carried out in California after the 1984 Olympics. Gary Condit was a state assemblyman campaigning for more to be done to address steroid use. His office wrote in 1985: 'If the abuse by world class athletes isn't frightening enough, evidence now shows that such abuse has filtered down below the high-school level to children and young teenagers.'[16] Steroid use was becoming politicized, attracting the attention of high-level politicians, which would lead to national legislation in many countries. Perhaps unsurprisingly, there were concerns over the nature and extent of the black market for steroids in the USA. The conviction of Jenkins and his crew of dealers in 1987 indicated the growth of this market, and by 1990 it was estimated to be worth over $300 million per year in the USA alone.[17]

Another indication of doping innovation and the accompanying challenges for sports authorities stemmed from the hugely successful American team at the 1984 Olympics. *Sports Illustrated* first covered the story in January 1985, but it was front-page news in *Rolling Stone* magazine in February 1985, reaching a much wider audience. The headline read 'AN OLYMPIC SCANDAL:

How u.s. Medalists Were Doped to Win' and the article itself was titled 'Olympic Cheating: The Inside Story of Illicit Doping and the u.s. Cycling Team'. It transpired that the cycling coach had organized a blood-transfusion system, otherwise known as blood doping. Seven cyclists took part, including four medal winners.

Blood doping had been identified in a handful of cases, mostly track and field athletes and cyclists, but up to 1985 there had not been much outcry about this method. That might have been because the scientific community was uncertain as to whether or not it was effective for enhancement. The removal, freezing and re-insertion of blood could help boost red blood cells, leading to improved recovery and performance. Another option was to use another person's blood. The IOC had not given the technique much attention, and there was no test for it. In 1982 de Merode said: 'Our position [that of the IOC Medical Commission] is that it [blood transfusions] should not exist. We cannot prevent it, but we can point out that it is dangerous.'[18] However, the IOC would ban blood transfusions in the aftermath of the publicity even though a test for such practices was unavailable and would not be available for another fifteen years. The sports historian John Gleaves argued that the u.s. cycling blood-doping case in 1985 had ramifications far beyond the athletes involved, and even beyond the IOC decision to ban that specific method. Instead, it ushered in a new determination to identify and sanction dopers:

Following the 1984 Games, the previously cautious Medical Commission, who feared backlash from doping controversy, became bullish in their mindset. The 'ban first, test later' approach and the ambiguously inclusive language indicated a galvanised Medical Commission now intent on eradicating doping of any kind in sport. The Medical Commission interpreted the emerging high octane Olympic sport to mean that athletes would willingly push all available boundaries in their pursuit of 'higher, faster, stronger'. With this new attitude, the commission would soon flex its muscles. At the next Olympic Games, held in 1988 in Seoul, South Korea, the IOC would strip Canadian Ben Johnson of his gold medal in the marquee 100-meter track event. This unprecedented move of stripping a high profile athlete during the Games marked a new approach to doping that had been put in place in the wake of the U.S. cycling team's employment of blood transfusions at the 1984 Games. This approach, which illustrates part of the lasting legacy of the 1984 Los Angeles Olympic Games, has continuously remained in place in the three decades since *Rolling Stone* scandalised the U.S. cycling team's use of blood transfusions.[19]

Ben Johnson: The Olympic Scandal that Changed Public Perceptions

The name Ben Johnson is synonymous with the history of doping. He was at the centre of the biggest scandal in sport up to that point. Indeed, his was the biggest scandal in the Olympics until the Lance Armstrong evidence was published in 2012 and the years-long Russian doping system was exposed in the months leading up to the 2016 Games. Johnson has been the subject of various documentaries and books, and his story is widely known. He was a Jamaican-born Canadian sprinter coached by Charlie Francis, who introduced him to steroids in 1981. He was arch-rivals with the American Carl Lewis in the years preceding the 1988 Olympics, where their clash came to a head. The 100-metre final was highly anticipated, in no small part due to their rivalry. Johnson was a popular figure and admired by fellow athletes and fans.

As we have discussed, steroids had been a part of sport for around two decades at this point. They first showed up in strength sports before moving into track and field. Francis had known about

steroids in athletics since the early 1970s, had used them himself and had developed a sophisticated understanding of how to
effectively use them with the support of Jamie Astaphan and the
massage therapist Waldemar Matuszewski. Steroids were easy to
access in Canada and one regular source of supply was the shot
putter Bishop Dolegiewicz, among others. It was later revealed
that Johnson was not tested between February 1988 and the date
of his positive test in September 1988. He had passed nineteen
tests between 1986 and 1988, but had never been tested outside of
competition.[20] For several years preceding the Olympics Canadian
athletes and officials suspected that Francis's close-knit group
of sprinters were using steroids. Both male and female athletes
showed significant changes in their performances and their phys-
iques after joining his group. Some athletes refused to join his
group because they did not want to use drugs. Yet the speculation and whistle-blower evidence did not lead to any investigation
or additional testing. Francis would later admit that he thought
steroids were necessary to compete at the highest level in sport.

Johnson's positive test was not the result of a small-scale
operation in Canada. It was the consequence of a systematic
failure of sports organizations, national and international, to
confront the issue. There was no testing outside of competitions
and very few in-competition tests, and the sanctions for being
caught were not enough to deter users. Once broader patterns
of use developed and methods for avoiding the testers became
known, the logical response was – as Francis said – to join in this
performance-enhancing culture.

A curious aspect of Johnson's positive result was why it happened. The initial response from Johnson and Francis was to deny
taking any steroids at all. Johnson claimed a stranger entered the
changing room after the race and might have spiked his drink. The
IOC scientists said that the amount of the banned drug – stanozolol – in his sample showed longer-term use, so they abandoned

that explanation. Later Francis would admit that Johnson was using a number of steroids but stanozolol was not among them. It is possible that Johnson ignored Francis's advice and used the drug himself without an understanding of the excretion rate. However, that seems unlikely given how closely monitored he was and that he was on a sophisticated regime of substances. Another possibility is that a mistake was made either in the sample collection process or the scientific analysis. These were checked by Canadian investigators and found to be correct. Johnson and his teammates were given a last short regime of drugs a month before the Seoul Olympics, none of which were stanozolol according to those involved, and they were given diuretic drugs to help mask the steroids.[21] The subsequent examination of all the participants concluded that Astaphan had been giving the athletes stanozolol without their knowledge:

> Notwithstanding his protestations to the contrary, I am satisfied that when Dr Astaphan introduced 'estragol' to his athlete patients in 1985, he was in fact administering stanozolol and that, even more disturbing, the stanozolol he was administering was the injectable Winstrol-V which he had purchased from Sterling Drug Ltd. I am also satisfied that Dr Astaphan never told the athletes that the drug he was providing to them was in fact a veterinary product.[22]

It appears from this that the mistake was in giving athletes a short course of drugs before the Games and not disclosing that one of the drugs involved was stanozolol, even though it was assumed that Francis was aware that it was being used. Fellow sprinter Angella Taylor-Issajenko discussed Johnson's positive with teammate Desai Williams: 'And Desai said to me that he did not believe it was sabotage. He said I [Williams] passed with twenty-eight days at the Nationals, I gave it twenty-eight days here, and I just think Ben and Jamie cut it too close.' In this view, the mistake was in the timing, perhaps only by a day or two. Or it was possibly in the over-confidence of administering drugs only a month before the test without having a good pre-screening process in place.

Regardless of the missteps that led to it, Johnson's positive test gave the IOC the opportunity to make a huge public statement about doping. They had become the leaders in this field, regularly gathering together skilled scientific advisers and having a clearly defined list of banned substances. The allegations surrounding the 1984 Olympics no doubt emboldened those in charge, and they had the support of the Executive Board to make decisions. It was also rare to get a positive test for steroids at a major competition, much less one so high-profile or for such a widely publicized event. For those scientists, officials and anti-doping campaigners who saw a much higher moral purpose in the Olympics that was being degraded by doping – and who wanted to protect athletes' health – this was a golden opportunity to promote their cause. It would usher in demands for regular out-of-competition testing and more accredited laboratories. Reputations were being made and empires being built.

Of course, the 1988 Olympics was full of athletes who had doped in preparation for the event. The USSR topped the table with 55 gold medals, 31 silver and 46 bronze. East Germany was second with 37 gold, 35 silver and 30 bronze in what would be its last Olympics. The USA was third with 36 gold, 31 silver and 27 bronze. The estimates of how many athletes were using steroids vary, and can only ever be a rough guess. It seems probable that almost all the East Germans were in the doping programme, but they only used one drug, Oral Turinabol, and did not move to drugs such as growth hormones that they did not have much knowledge about. North American and European athletes had access to a much wider array of drugs. In 1989 the American coach Pat Connolly said that at least fifteen out of fifty track and field athletes in the

1984 Olympics had used steroids. She estimated that around 40 per cent of the female u.s. track and field athletes had used them for the 1988 Olympics.[23]

Doping was both everywhere and nowhere: the evidence from rumours, improved performances and changing body shapes suggested that steroids were integral to many sports; the definitive evidence from positive tests was rare. This gulf led to speculation, including media coverage offering sweeping generalizations that could neither be confirmed nor refuted. Governments and public health officials were increasingly concerned about elite athletes as role models influencing young and amateur athletes whose usage could not be controlled through rules, testing and bans from sport – and, indeed, whose health risks were much higher than those of elite athletes who consulted expert doping doctors. Into this fluid space of uncertainty stepped investigators and policy analysts intent on understanding the problem in more detail.

Responses to the Johnson Scandal

Following Johnson's 1988 scandal, the Canadian Government launched a full inquiry, the Dubin Inquiry, into doping within their country. During the hearings 46 athletes admitted using steroids. The broader context was not forgotten by the leader of the inquiry and author of the final report, Charles Dubin:

> After hearing the evidence and meeting with knowledgeable people from Canada, the United States, the United Kingdom, Australia, New Zealand, and elsewhere, I am convinced that the problem is widespread not only in Canada but also around the world. The evidence shows that banned performance-enhancing substances and, in particular, anabolic steroids are being used by athletes in almost every sport, most extensively in weightlifting and track and field.[24]

Evidence of steroid use was starting to emerge from other countries. Then-Senator Joe Biden led a u.s. Senate Judiciary Committee Hearing on Steroid Abuse in America in April 1989. The health risks of steroids were beginning to be publicized. The athlete Diane Williams wept while telling the Committee that during her steroid use she had grown a moustache and stopped menstruating, even as her clitoris grew to 'embarrassing proportions . . . I am greatly concerned if I will ever be able to bear a normal child . . . I have been experiencing . . . intense itching, sore mouth, higher sex drive, depression, vaginal bleeding and, most of all, lower abdominal pain.'[25] Congress passed the Anabolic Steroids Control Act in 1990 to classify the drugs as a controlled substance and thus criminalized trafficking. By this time Dan Duchaine had been imprisoned and released, serving ten months of a five-year sentence. In 1991, while still on probation, he was caught selling GHB (gamma-hydroxybutyrate) for muscle building. One of his customers, however, was an undercover Food and Drug Administration (FDA) agent, and Duchaine was convicted a second time and sentenced to 36 months in prison.[26]

The Australian government established a Senate standing committee in 1988 for investigating steroid use led by Senator John Black. The committee heard that approximately 70 per cent of Australian athletes who competed internationally had used steroids, and that around 25 per cent of the Australian track and field team who competed in Seoul had also done so.[27] At the time, the black market for steroids in Australia had been estimated as worth anywhere between $15 million and $150 million a year.

Within the sports community there was now a determined effort to organize testing processes. Ironically, the First Permanent World Conference on Anti-Doping in Sport had been held in Canada in July 1988, just before the start of the Olympics. The conference brought together international experts to discuss potential solutions. There were 85 delegates from 27 countries, including the USSR, East Germany, China and South Korea. Between them, they created a twenty-page International Anti-Doping Charter to be presented to the IOC for its approval at the Seoul Olympics in September.[28]

The Ben Johnson scandal led to heightened awareness of the issues in Canada and globally. On his return home, he faced a media scrum at the airport and wide-scale criticism, even being labelled a 'national embarrassment' by the sports minister Jean Charest. At the same time, Edwin Moses said: 'This will change the history of the Olympics . . . This will change a lot of people's lives.'[29] If he meant the introduction of rigorous testing, then he would be correct, though it would take several more years to get a system in place. Johnson faced a ban from sport for the rest of his life and demanded a formal inquiry that would put his positive test within the context of the global failure to prevent doping. This would become the Dubin Inquiry, which was formally titled the 'Royal Commission to Inquire into the Use of Drugs and Banned Practices Intended to Increase Athletic Performance' and reported on 26 June 1990. However, the various testimonies included had already been publicized – the admissions from Charlie Francis, Johnson and others were covered by newspapers from early 1989 onwards.

The Council of Europe, whose conference in 1963 had proved influential in the making of early policies, responded again, this time with a formal Anti-Doping Convention. While this did not mandate any specific policy implementation, it clearly shows the emerging demands for a globalized response to doping. Published on 16 November 1989, it was signed by 48 governments, including some outside of Europe such as Australia, Canada, Belarus and Tunisia. This was a detailed document with the overall aims of protecting athletes' health and the fairness of competition, and encouraging signatories to take responsibility. These were summarized in the Convention: 'to take further and stronger co-operative action aimed at the reduction and eventual elimination of doping in sport using as a basis the ethical values and practical measures contained in those instruments'.[30] In brief, it encouraged signatories to undertake a collective approach that included education, restricting supply, testing and working with accredited laboratories. In some ways, this was the beginning of the bureaucratization of anti-doping. There were nineteen articles presented in formal, almost legalistic language, making anti-doping into a regulated policy process with the associated baggage of rules, recommendations, roles and responsibilities and procedures. There was always the risk of de-humanizing anti-doping by forgetting that at the heart of the matter lie athletes whose motivations, experiences and values both explain and determine patterns of doping and anti-doping.

The world of sport was still some way off from a fully harmonized approach, and little was done to resolve the issue of standardizing bans, with the implication that governments could work with their own national sports organizations to carry out anti-doping. However, along with the conference held in Canada before the Olympics, we see a movement towards globalization that goes above and beyond the IOC and the Olympics, and that attempted to develop a framework that could be applied to all sports in all countries. It was also the first time that it was made clear that out-of-competition testing should be in place:

> the Parties shall encourage their sports organisations . . . to introduce, on an effective scale, doping controls not only at, but also without advance warning at any appropriate time outside, competitions, such controls to be conducted in a way which is equitable for all sportsmen and sportswomen and which include testing and retesting of persons selected, where appropriate, on a random basis.[31]

This is similar to one of Charles Dubin's recommendations in the published 1990 report:

> That doping controls be weighted towards unannounced out-of-competition testing. Because of the difficulties of conducting tests without notice in a large country like Canada, it is recommended that the Sport Medicine Council of Canada establish a mixture of techniques including without-notice, short-notice, and targeted tests. The out-of-competition tests should also be weighted towards high-risk sports.[32]

Therefore, we see that by 1990 major stakeholder organizations, governments and inquiries had recommended a more stringent approach towards controlling the supply of doping substances than had been previously attempted. This included increasing the volume and frequency of testing and having a globally agreed strategy. It would be another ten years before a single organization was established to take these ideas forward. For the rest of the 1990s anti-doping rules remained somewhat vague, insubstantial, inconsistent and fragmented. Indeed, with hindsight, there was an inertia about anti-doping, as if the response to a scandal could not be maintained and applied through periods without scandal. Shock and panic led to action, short-term rather than long-term, and policies came and went in line with media coverage and public interest.

The East German System Revealed

However, a second global event kicked off a chain of events that would significantly influence perceptions of doping and the need for increased anti-doping controls: the fall of the Berlin Wall in November 1989 led to the demise of East Germany and the gradual revelations around the country's doping programme. The first signs of news about this programme appeared in the media in the months preceding the political revolution. In June and July 1989 the West German newspaper *Bild am Sonntag* ran an eight-part series based on interviews with two defectors who had escaped East Germany: Hans-Georg Aschenbach and Hans-Juergen Noczenski. Aschenbach was a four-time world champion ski jumper and a gold medal winner at the 1976 Winter Olympics who then became a doctor in one of the elite sports academies. Noczenski had been the chairman of the East German Judo Federation.

Their interviews described a wide-scale and abusive system. The headline read: 'Olympic Champion Divulges Biggest Sports Scandal; All East German Stars Doped; Also Katarina Witt'. The allegations were summarized in the *Los Angeles Times*:

> All East German athletes are force-fed performance-enhancing drugs, such as anabolic steroids, beginning as early as age 13 in some sports, including figure skating, gymnastics and swimming . . . Aschenbach said the young athletes initially are told that the drugs are vitamins. Those who balk when they eventually learn the truth, he said, no longer are allowed to compete internationally, lose membership in their sports clubs and are harassed in their private lives . . . athletes are closely watched by the state police, who monitor their telephone calls and mail and maintain files regarding their personal lives.[33]

More evidence came to light following these initial reports. Christiane Knacke was a 100-metre butterfly specialist who had defected to Austria. She won silver in the 1977 European Championships and bronze at the 1980 Olympics. She broke the world record to become the first female to swim the 100 metres in less than a minute. She told a newspaper that she had been forced to take steroids, and that she blamed those drugs for the health problems later suffered by her daughter.

The full extent of doping was revealed in 1991 when the documents of the programme came into the public domain. Those leading the excavation included Brigitte Berendonk, who published a book in German in 1991 that reproduced records – *Doping Dokumente* – discovered at the sports training academies. Berendonk competed in the shot put at the 1968 and 1972 Olympics after she defected from East Germany with her parents as a teenager in 1958. She campaigned to reveal the nature and scope of the East German doping system along with her husband, the scientist Werner Franke, and subsequently with other researchers. Franke was commissioned by the new German government in 1990 to investigate the doping system.

As the news began to seep out to the international domain, Franke gave startling accounts of what had gone on in the East German state. For example, he told the *Washington Post* in 1991: 'The government took control of the bodies of children as if they were its personal property.' He went on to note that the young athletes were not told what they were being given: 'They just were told to take one blue one, one yellow one and so forth.' They were also told not to tell their families. Some athletes were as young as thirteen, and problematic side effects were ignored by the coaches and doctors.[34]

Stories of athletes who suffered from the consequences of doping, especially female athletes, would continue to come out through the mid-1990s. The leaders of the doping system were prosecuted in the German re-unification trials, and over two hundred athletes testified against them. This evidence worked to shift concerns about doping to focus on health rather than cheating. There was further scrutiny of the abuse athletes suffered rather than on the athletes choosing to intentionally dope. While Charles Dubin established that Johnson and other athletes knew they were engaged in a programme of steroids, the emphasis in the discussion of East Germany was upon what the athletes themselves did not know.

The scandal also worked as a critique of the closed communist state with its highly powered secret police, a state that had abused its own citizens in other ways. The critique of doping fitted into the post-communist glasnost era, another sign that the 'evil empire' needed to change. However, the news of these stories was drip-fed to the public throughout the 1990s as the trials dragged to a conclusion in 2000. Individual accounts of physiological and psychological health problems served to support the overall critique. Since then, East Germany has been regularly referred to as an example of what can happen if doping is left uncontrolled.

The East German system was certainly different from the individualized Western culture of doping. It was organized at the highest levels of government. Formal studies of the substances were conducted in the 1960s and used to inform dosages. The drugs were obtained from the state pharmaceutical company and distributed through doctors and coaches within the system. Each athlete had a tailored programme linked to their training and the events they were aiming to compete in, and side effects were assumed to be short-term. Athletes were either not told what they were taking or were not given a choice about whether to take them. Samples were tested before international events to ensure there were no positives. Any 'accidental' positives led to a hasty withdrawal and an internal investigation. Yet there was none of the self-experimentation, poly-drug use, dependence on unreliable suppliers and risky innovation that was happening in other countries at this time. And there is no evidence that East German high-school, non-elite or recreational bodybuilders could access these drugs.

Unlike previous investigations into widespread doping, however, the investigations into the East German system revealed that athletes suffered a wide range of side effects. These were summarized by Franke and Berendonk in a 1997 research paper:

Muscle tightness, body weight increase, muscle cramps, irregular menstruation including amenorrhea, acne, alteration of libido, sexual potency and fertility, edema, diarrhea and constipation, liver damage, deaths (3), gynecomastopathy, severe liver damage requiring hospitalization, excessive hirsutism, Polycystic ovarian syndrome, deepening of voice, nymphomania, loss of libido (in males), arrest of body growth (in adolescents).[35]

These effects seemed to be mirrored in some Western cases. One in particular was that of the West German heptathlete Birgit Dressel, who died aged 26 in 1987. She had taken over one hundred medications, some of which appear to have been banned substances, including steroids. She went into toxic shock and died after three days in hospital.[36] Many experts, including Werner Franke, blamed her overuse of steroids. When former East German athletes told the courts and the media that they had suffered organ damage and psychological trauma and had given birth to children with physical deformities, it seemed that the over-arching concern would be to prevent such abuse from happening again. Yet the Olympics in 1992 and 1996 passed without another scandal, though accusations were made of another IOC cover-up in 1996. As we will see in the next chapter, there were several complex legal cases in the UK and the USA that would further illustrate the need for a consistent approach to testing and sanctioning athletes.

Cultures of Performance Enhancement

The years between the 1984 Olympics and the revelations of East German doping would mark the end of innocence for those who imagined sport was clean. Later investigations would expose a highly organized approach to doping in West Germany, and there is some whistle-blower evidence of doping in China in the late 1980s and early 1990s. This was also the era that ushered in new commercial opportunities which made athletes household names and potentially millionaires. The expansion of media coverage of the sports events and the amount paid by broadcasters to the IOC to show the Olympics was increasing every quadrennial. Professional team sports were seeing similar expansions, leading to global audiences.

Yet, in the haste to develop new methods of controlling doping practices, there was very little in the way of reflection on the causes of doping. Throughout the 1970s and '80s there was a Cold War rivalry in which neither side wanted to restrict their athletes' ability to win medals. However, in the post-Cold War era, and with the widely accepted view that Olympic athletes could be professionals and could use a range of performance-enhancing measures, anti-doping tried to draw a line between what was fair and healthy and what was not.

The Ben Johnson scandal and the East German stories of young girls being force-fed male hormone steroids shocked the sports world into supporting enhanced anti-doping controls. Simplistic educational messages circulated about the dangers of doping. Experts met regularly to find ways of improving surveillance and increasing punishments. Event organizers, national sports ministers and journalists all supported the anti-doping movement. Yet doping continued within elite sport and bodybuilding, and at lower levels of competitive sport. New methods such as blood doping and undetectable drugs like EPO were becoming widely used in a range of sports, and the lack of clarity over legal processes would open up some prolonged appeals processes, both of which we discuss in the next chapter. All this led to a moral panic response as the officials charged with leading anti-doping took a 'war on drugs' perspective that would lead to some innocent athletes receiving harsh penalties. This reaction was supported by an increasingly powerful bureaucracy and would result in a long list of unintended consequences. From the early 1980s momentum was building towards a globalized, systematic and consistent policy approach. This would emerge in the early 2000s, but it would be the events of the 1990s that made a draconian, uncompromising, top-down approach inevitable.

6

Facing Up to the Scandals

The 1990s was the decade in which doping stories grew larger and more complex, while the anti-doping policy system looked increasingly incapable of keeping a lid on the problem.

Several global changes outside of sport were making the situation more critical. First, former communist countries were opening their borders. Within sport, this was a double-edged sword: it meant that anti-doping organizations could penetrate previously closed states, but it also meant that coaches from East Germany, the USSR and other Eastern European countries were free to move to other countries with their expertise of perform-ance enhancement methods. Athletes who had been part of the East German doping system were now eligible to represent the reunified Germany. Second, with more political emphasis on free trade, both official and unofficial suppliers of enhancement pharmaceuticals took advantage of new opportunities. The legiti-mate anti-ageing industry that used hormone therapies under medical supervision began taking off during this decade. Despite the rapid growth of these legal methods, the black market for ster-oids in the USA was worth an estimated $300 million by 1990.[1] Third, the rewards for success within sport were ramping up due to an influx of media and sponsorship money. The days of Cold War rivalries driving Olympic competitiveness were replaced with an individualistic approach for career success, and countries from the Global South encouraged their athletes to seek the rewards while bringing glory to their nations. The globalization and commercialization of sport had implications for the doping trade and opportunities for suppliers looking to help athletes enhance their performance. However, globalization also led to challenges for governments and international sports bodies that sought to keep doping under control. The scandals of the 1980s would prove the precursor for a turbulent 1990s.

The decade started with the most famous footballer in the world, Diego Maradona, being banned twice for doping. The second ban effectively ended his career. There was also the aftermath of the end of the East German state that saw reunification with West Germany and an attempt to prosecute the criminals of the former communist state in the newly unified German courts. The trials of the programme's architects, Manfred Ewald and Manfred Höppner, gave former athletes a platform for testifying about the drugs they were given as young athletes and the health impacts they suffered as a result. Global media covered the story and presented further interviews with athletes. The devastatingly abusive nature of East German sports fed into the wider understanding of doping as evil and unforgivable and media stories continued in other countries about doping in elite sport. As the decade progressed, it became clear that international sports organizations needed to find better answers to the challenging questions posed by the evidence of systematic of sport doping cultures.

Yet there were some more ambivalent situations. Steroid use had become normalized in bodybuilding in previous decades, but this subculture was increasingly marginalized as fitness culture commercialized and expanded to include more diverse groups. Natural or drug-free bodybuilding also emerged in this decade, though steroid use remained widespread. In sport, anti-doping decisions did not always strike the optimal targets. The tighter the rules became, the more cases emerged of athletes who were banned from sport due to laboratory mistakes, contaminated supplements or even taking the wrong medicine. Many of these cases bounced around sports tribunals and criminal courts as jurisdictions were unclear. The decade ended with the extraordinary Tour de France scandal in 1998, which – along with other factors – proved the catalyst for the IOC to organize a conference in November 1999 during which governments and sports organizations agreed to create the World Anti-Doping Agency (WADA).

A sense of crisis emerged in response to these scandals and led to global demand for a tougher system at the end of the decade. Ironically, this came just as other forms of drug policy were beginning to turn away from the harmful 'war on drugs' approach and towards more pragmatic policies, such as harm reduction and even decriminalization in some places. Sport has moved along a punitive vector of substance regulation ever since: steadfastly hanging on to the clean sport message, punishing any infraction of rules with bans stigmatizing those who are caught for the duration of their career and beyond. The groundwork for WADA's uncompromising approach was laid in the 1990s as fears of widespread and abusive doping cultures framed the debate, bolstered by episodic evidence of health harms, and problems within the anti-doping policy environment that needed to be addressed.

The Perceived Risks of Steroids in Sport and Society

The public perception of doping ebbs and flows. A scandal makes doping news and creates drama, and sensationalized headlines underpinned by implications of corruption and bad behaviour capture the imagination and make for a good story. However, the more banal reality was that performance-enhancing drugs were seeping further into everyday life in many countries throughout the 1980s and '90s. Though this rarely made it into the headlines, this pattern was recognized by public health researchers as an emerging issue. Several surveys from this period highlighted the scale – and scope – of use.

One of the earliest of such studies was Rise Terney and Larry McLain's 1990 investigation of steroid use among u.s. high-school students.[2] They received 2,113 responses, of which 4.4 per cent admitted using steroids. The numbers were higher among males (6.5 per cent) and athletes (5.5 per cent). Published in the *Journal of Diseases in Children*, it positioned steroid use as a potential threat to be discussed alongside other paediatric health concerns. The authors noted: 'These data suggest that we have another serious, as yet unappreciated drug problem in our adolescents.'[3] This was the same year that trafficking of steroids was criminalized in the usa. Additionally, health policy researcher Charles Yesalis and colleagues used the 1991 National Household Survey on Drug Abuse to describe the patterns of steroid use in the usa. They reported that over 1 million people were current or former users and around 300,000 had used steroids within the previous year. This paper associated steroid use with other social harms. The authors reported that steroid use was linked to the use of other illicit drugs, cigarettes, alcohol, aggressive behaviour and crimes against property.[4] It was published in the high-profile and influential *Journal of the American Medical Association*.

Three surveys from the uk showed how knowledge and understanding of steroid use was being developed and framed. A study in Wales conducted in 1992 on members of private gyms found that from a sample of three hundred individuals, 39 per cent had used steroids. The most common of these were Dianabol (metandienone), Deca-Durabolin (nandrolone), testosterone and stanozolol. Despite the authors' lack of specific research questions about health in the data collection process, they discussed potential risks and the article's title hinted at more troubling outcomes: 'Dying to Be Big: A Review of Anabolic Steroid Use'.[5] In a 1993 survey Williamson focused on a single further education college and found that 2.8 per cent of 687 technology college students reported previously or currently using steroids, again finding prevalence higher among male students (4.4 per cent).[6] Despite the small number of respondents, the author highlighted the broader implications:

> The overall rate of current or previous use of anabolic steroids was 2.8% (4.4% in males, 1.0% in females). Of these, 56% had first used anabolic steroids at age 15 or less. Anabolic steroid users were more likely to be male, under 17 years of age, and participating in bodybuilding, weight-lifting or rugby. The results of this survey, if confirmed in other groups of young people, would suggest that use of anabolic steroids may be widespread in the UK.[7]

Steroid use in the UK had become a concern for the government by the mid-1990s, and a national survey was commissioned by the Department of Health for England, Scotland and Wales. From a sample of 1,667 respondents, the authors reported that 9.1 per cent of men and 2.3 per cent of women had used steroids in the past and that 6 per cent of men and 1.4 per cent of women were current users. Although side effects were only reported among a small minority of respondents, they included a wide range of disorders: testicular atrophy, kidney and liver disfunction, gynaecomastia (among men), elevated blood pressure, fluid retention, injuries to tendons, nosebleeds, more frequent colds, sleep problems and (among women) menstrual irregularity, clitoral enlargement and decreased breast size. Thus we see steroid use being interwoven with a range of health issues, even if the scale of the problem was relatively unknown. To discuss the side effects, the authors interviewed 97 users and some issues were only experienced by a handful of users.[8] Nonetheless, it contributed to the developing themes in government and medical research: steroids were bad news and use needed to be controlled.

The perception of an emerging threat fed into wider social anxieties about steroids that crossed over from elite sport to youth sport to non-sport contexts. The optimistic visions of the hormone therapy pioneers of the 1940s and '50s had given way to fears of drug abuse cultures, health side effects and the hyper-masculinization of women (despite much lower use among women). The knowledge gained through surveys and anecdotes was patchy and incomplete, based on localized surveys and very few clinical trials. Given the unclear nature of the evidence base, it was almost impossible to separate the risks of steroid use from related risks, including over-training with heavy weights, dietary issues, use of other drugs and medicines, overuse of steroids, poly-steroid use and poor hygiene practices (sharing needles, cross-contamination, unsterile environments). Any chance of harm minimization strategies being proposed – which would accept the reality of steroid use and offer support to users – was derailed by the news from East Germany. The gradual emergence of horrific stories from women given steroids at a young age would add another pillar of support to the critical view of steroids and revitalize the demands for prohibition policies in sport.

Challenging Cases

The 1992 Olympics may have passed over with no major anti-doping scandals, no doubt to the relief of the IOC after Ben Johnson's 1988 scandal, but a range of new drugs had come onto the market and were being used by athletes. An example of this developing pharmacology was clenbuterol, which athletes started using in the late 1980s because it was not banned. However, several cases of clenbuterol use during the 1992 Games highlighted the struggles faced by the IOC in keeping up with the performance innovators. Indeed, the rules on clenbuterol were not clear as it was initially assumed to be a stimulant before being moved into the anabolic steroid category. The IOC did announce a ban on clenbuterol several months before the start of the 1992 Games. However, up to that point its status had been unclear:

> As a stimulant with anabolic qualities, Clenbuterol has had an ambiguous standing with sports authorities. The drug had not been listed by name on the list of substances banned by the International Amateur Athletic Federation, the world body for track and field. It was included implicitly under a general listing for 'related' substances that are illegal for use.[9]

One of the athletes found to have used it was the shot putter Bonnie Dasse, who admitted taking the drug on the advice of her friend three days before her competition started. This demonstrated a lack of knowledge about the IOC's policies on prohibited substances, their use and the testing system within the athletic community. Dasse was disqualified and this ended her career. After he finished fourth in the hammer event, American athlete Jud Logan also tested positive for the drug. He claimed to have used it as a safer alternative to steroids for five months, but said that he stopped taking it four months before the Games after the IOC announced it was banned. There was also some confusion over an asthma medication he was taking. Ultimately, the IOC made the decision to disqualify Logan and send him home. The IOC had no authority for any further ban, as that responsibility was left to the relevant sports authorities. However, there is no evidence he was given any sanction.[10] The British delegation also sent home two weightlifters after it was discovered they had used clenbuterol before the Games started. This prompted some intense deliberation when members of the British Olympic Association were unclear whether it was right to send them home given the lack of clarity over when they had used it and the rules. They were subsequently cleared by the British Weightlifting Association of any offence, not given any ban, and one of them went on to coach an Olympian at the 2008 Games in Beijing.[11] The ioc's lack of consistent rules was further highlighted in the case of Katrin Krabbe, for whom a positive test for the same substance had much more significance. The German runner tested positive just before the 1992 Games started and therefore did not compete. She was subsequently banned for one year by the German Athletics Association, plus two additional years by the IAAF. She did not compete in international events again following these sanctions. After a lengthy legal battle arguing against this 'double jeopardy' she received financial compensation in 2002 from the IAAF of £378,850 plus 4 per cent interest for the period since 1994.[12]

Two years after those Olympics, a positive anti-doping test for ephedrine ended the international career of the Argentinian footballer Diego Maradona, widely considered one of the best players of the sport ever. Maradona had previously been banned for fifteen months for using cocaine while playing for Napoli. Testing positive for and receiving a ban for cocaine continues to be a controversial issue, as cocaine is not usually taken to enhance sport performance. Many athletes have used it recreationally and testing has been variable across sports. From the 1970s until the 1990s some sports did not have any regulations prohibiting using cocaine and, as such, they were not testing players for it. As will be discussed in the next chapter, WADA later attempted to install a more consistent approach but that still resulted in athletes receiving sanctions ranging from a simple warning to a full four-year ban for a first offence. Maradona's positive test for cocaine, and other issues including tax payments, meant that he left Napoli in 1992. He had played there since 1984, during which time he established himself on the national stage by winning two Italian League titles, as well as cups and competition trophies, and on the international stage in the 1986 and 1990 World Cups. The 1986 World Cup is, of course, renowned for Maradona's Hand of God goal and incredible second goal against England, and his captaining of Argentina to the World Cup win. He was captain again in 1990, losing the final 1–0 to West Germany.

At the 1994 World Cup Maradona scored a goal against Greece. He celebrated by running close to a TV camera with exuberance, his eyes bulging and his face contorted in delirious delight. FIFA sent him home after he tested positive in a post-match doping control. While ephedrine is banned because it is a stimulant, it is also found in some cold medicines and even supplements. Maradona later claimed that his coach recommended a nutritional supplement called Rip Fuel. He said the U.S. version contained ephedrine but the Argentinian version did not, a mistake that could lead to unintentionally ingesting the substance. He also argued that FIFA had given him permission to use the supplement to help with losing weight. Even if the player and the coach had failed to be vigilant enough, these two controversial anti-doping cases cast a tragic shadow over Maradona's career. The scandals ultimately forced his retirement, first from European club football and then from the Argentinian national team.

The consequences of his fall from grace were best summed up by Scottish journalist Hugh McIlvanney:

It was the grubby tumult of an unscheduled press conference in Dallas on Thursday evening that most effectively conveyed the sadness seeping through the squalor of Diego Maradona's expulsion from the World Cup. As a mass of hands holding microphones closed around him like a carnivorous plant, the drawn, slightly hunted look on his Spanish-Indian face said more about the nature and origins of his predicament than the predictable words of denial and complaint that came from his mouth.[13]

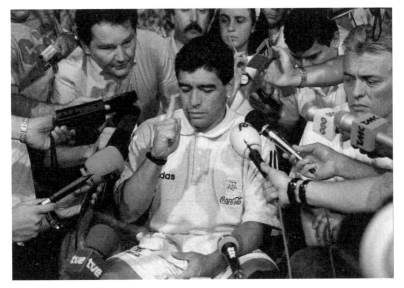

Diego Maradona after testing positive during the 1994 World Cup.

In a much less widely publicized case that same year was a traumatic instance of an athlete wrongly accused of doping. Diane Modahl (then Edwards) was a successful English middle-distance runner – she won the gold medal in the 800 metres at the 1990 Commonwealth Games – who fell victim to inadequate standards of anti-doping testing. Following her 1990 Commonwealth Games gold, Modahl came fourth in the World Championships in 1993, and was having a good season in the run up to the 1994 Olympic Games. She returned a positive sample at the 1994 athletics World Championships in Lisbon, leading to her being excluded from the Commonwealth Games later that year. After a prolonged legal battle, and with the support of scientists at the University of Manchester, she managed to prove that her urine sample had degraded after being left on a table in a room for three days at over 35 degrees. This, the scientists showed, could lead to a false positive. Moreover, the laboratory had tried to invent chain of custody documents and had wrongly processed a sample with a pH value of 8.85 (it was originally 5) despite the IOC rules that a sample with pH higher than 7.5 should not be processed. On this basis, Modahl won her appeal and her ban was lifted in June 1995. However, her story was far from over. She went on to launch further legal challenges seeking to recover her legal costs. This process went on for six years and, by the time she lost the case, bankrupted both herself and the British Athletics Federation. Modahl did make a return to sport and competed in her fourth consecutive Olympics in 2000, but never fulfilled her earlier promise. She detailed the emotional turmoil and stress of the doping situation in her autobiography, which at the worst point led her to contemplate suicide. She reflected on her shock, feelings of loss, sense of injustice and hopelessness, writing: 'During the eleven months of my ordeal I'd contemplated suicide more than once . . . if the verdict went against me, I felt I had nothing left to live for and no will to go on.'[14]

Another world-leading athlete who faced a complex anti-doping accusation was American middle-distance runner Mary Decker. Decker had a famous rivalry with South African Zola Budd in the 1980s. She won two golds at the 1983 World Championships (1,500 metres and 3,000 metres), and over the course of a stellar career she broke seventeen world records, including being the first woman athlete to run the mile under four minutes and twenty seconds. She had been the favourite for the 1984 Olympics 3,000-metres event, but fell after becoming tangled with other runners in the final and did not finish the race. Her doping positive came more than a decade later in 1996, just ahead of the Atlanta Olympic Games. Her testosterone level was higher than the permitted 6:1 ratio of testosterone to epitestosterone, which her lawyers argued could not be accurately judged for an older woman who had taken hormonal birth control pills for many years. However, the appeals process was arduous and prolonged. Decker was initially banned by the IAAF in June 1997 but was reinstated by USA Track & Field in September 1999. The IAAF did not let it go and took the case to arbitration, which ruled against Decker. She was subsequently stripped of the silver medal she had won in the 1,500 metres in the 1997 World Championships. In April 1999 she responded by suing both the IAAF and the U.S. Olympic Committee, which had run the test. The U.S. Court of Appeals decided it had no jurisdiction and could not overturn the ban.[15] The decision reflected the ongoing dilemma about which legal bodies could make decisions about sport anti-doping bans. This case also foreshadowed the dilemma that WADA would address just a few years later.

Raising the Stakes: EPO Can Kill

As we have already discussed, cycling has a long tradition of stimulant use. Drugs such as amphetamines would give the rider a quick boost of energy, help them to push past the fatigue of a long race or give them a burst of speed when required. Further evidence of this had been publicized by the Irish professional cyclist Paul Kimmage, who would later become an investigative journalist, in his 1990 book *Rough Ride*. This was one of the few accounts showing the day-to-day reality of stimulant use among professional cyclists. Testing and sanctions were still somewhat limited around this time. For example, two years before Kimmage's book was published, the winner of the Tour de France, Pedro Delgado, tested positive for probenecid, which could be used to mask steroid use. He claimed it was for medicinal purposes. Such was the disorganized nature of anti-doping and any system of enforcement that when the organizers asked him to leave the race, he refused and was allowed to continue competing. Other incidents of doping found riders were given a time penalty rather than a ban.

The science of doping in cycling had radically changed by the 1990s, led by a handful of specialist scientists focused on manipulating blood. The aftermath of the 1984 Olympics blood-doping scandal had not diminished the interest in this technique, and there was no method of detection. Blood doping was complicated in that blood had to be removed while the athlete was in a healthy state, stored and replaced when the athlete needed it for rapid recovery. Doing this during races was both logistically challenging and risky. Blood bags would need to be secretly stored on team buses and delivered to hotel rooms with the re-insertion equipment. The riders receiving these bags would also need to be skilled and careful enough to perform the infusion procedure without medical assistance.

A much easier way to boost red blood cell production was by using synthetic EPO (Erythropoietin), a substance that would become widely used through the 1990s and 2000s by endurance athletes in a range of sports, not just in cycling. First developed in 1977, synthetic EPO was developed to help treat anaemia with a medical drug called epoetin that was approved by the U.S. Food and Drug Administration in 1989 and in Europe from 1991 under the names Aranesp, Epogen, Eprex and NeoRecormon.[16] While EPO is naturally occurring, exogenous EPO is known as recombinant EPO or rhEPO. However, rhEPO was indistinguishable from naturally occurring EPO so finding a scientific solution to detect its use proved very challenging and a reliable test for rhEPO would not be developed until the early 2000s.

This more sophisticated and complex approach to doping required expert help. One of the leading doping doctors was an Italian named Francesco Conconi. Conconi spent much of his professional life working in an official capacity for the Italian Olympic Committee while secretly using his research to facilitate doping in cycling. In fact, he had been funded by the latter organization and the IOC (he was a member of the IOC's Medical Commission) to find a test to detect EPO use – money he then used for a series of experiments with doping substances for professional cycling teams. He discovered a way to dope and beat the tests by combining EPO with a blood thinner and human growth hormone.

Anti-doping expert Alessandro Donati estimated that up to 80 per cent of the main cycling teams were using Conconi's cocktail by the mid-1990s. He told a reporter, 'It is completely impossible to be competitive at the world level without using performance-boosting substances.' Gilles Delion, a former professional rider from France noted, 'You couldn't be among the world's 50 best riders if you didn't take EPO, and it's been that way for quite a while.'[17] Of course, hard evidence is not easy to uncover but the 1996 Tour de France winner Bjarne Riis was one of those under suspicion:

> Investigations across Europe uncovered EPO use by athletes in every imaginable sport, from skiing to football. In Italy, police found evidence that Riis may have been among riders treated with EPO in 1994 and 1995 by medical researchers under Professor Francesco Conconi at the University of Ferrara. Files seized by police officers contain blood test results for Riis during those years. His red blood-cell count leaps from a base level of 41 per cent to a staggering 56.3 per cent. Debilitating illness could have explained the increase, but Riis was one of the fittest men alive, winning races that required extraordinary physical resilience.[18]

EPO might have opened up new possibilities for cyclists and cycling performances, but it troubled authorities due to a number of fatalities claimed to have been caused by the drug. There have been many claims about the health risks posed by misuse. Clinical experts viewed the risks posed by EPO as serious, with one group of scientists writing: 'As with steroids and hGH, doping with EPO is often injected in supernormal doses that could cause increased blood viscosity, deep vein and coronary thromboses, cerebral thromboses, pulmonary embolism, arrhythmias, stroke and death.'[19] The idea that too much EPO was potentially fatal developed quickly as a number of cyclists' deaths during the 1980s and '90s were rumoured to be linked to the drug. Such was the consensus around this claim that sports psychiatrist David Baron and colleagues later wrote that EPO is 'one of the most deadly doping agents'.[20]

The perceived risks associated with EPO emerged quite early on in the life cycle of the drug's production and dissemination, with the earliest of the apparent fatalities coming in 1987. The Spanish social scientist Bernat Lopez has discussed in detail how this claim emerged and whether or not it is an accurate assessment of the events. Anti-doping journalists and scientists were keen to see the connection between the tragic deaths and EPO. A wide range of commentators – from media to clinical scientists – have repeated the claim that around twenty cyclists died between the late 1980s and early 1990s. Lopez showed that for a wide set of reasons, almost none of these sad deaths could logically be attributed to EPO. He called the claim a 'flagship myth' that conveniently supported the anti-doping movement.

Moreover, Lopez expressed surprise at how quickly these claims were picked up, repeated and not considered to require further investigation regarding the evidence or its sources. Even academics simply regurgitated commonly held views. More importantly for the sense of drama and urgency was the media's tendency to accept and inflate the scandal:

A search for journalistic texts reporting on these facts has been conducted using the LexisNexis database and accessing the online archives of some newspapers. Twenty-four news reports have been retrieved, 35 in addition to a chapter from the journalistic book by Paul Kimmage. An analysis of these texts reveals an even higher degree of dispersion and imprecision. The number of victims range from 'half a dozen' to 'around 40' (other figures mentioned: 7, 14, 15, 16, 17, 18, 24 and 34). The most often quoted countries of origin are again Holland and Belgium, but Spain, Germany and

Poland are also mentioned, with many texts simply referring to 'European' cyclists. And the time span can be as broad as 1970–1990, or as narrow as 1988–1990.[21]

Nonetheless, it was clear from examples of media coverage using expert testimony that EPO would be linked with these deaths. The *New York Times* ran a story in May 1991 saying that even though the evidence was 'anecdotal', the drug was linked with eighteen deaths in cycling. The story quoted Randy Eichner: 'There is no absolute proof, but there's so much smoke that most of us are convinced. You just don't get 18 deaths in 4 years, mysteriously, with 10 of them attributed to cardiac problems.' Another expert cited was Edmund Burke, manager of the 1984 United States Olympic cycling team that had used blood doping. 'You have to tell them, "EPO can do wonders for your aerobic capacity. The problem is, it can also kill you."' Moreover, the list of deaths seemed highly troubling if they were to be associated with EPO use, 'Physicians say they believe athletes began using the drug almost with the beginning of clinical trials in 1986. Then the deaths began. In 1987 five Dutch racers died suddenly. In 1988 a Belgian and two more Dutch riders died. In 1989 five more Dutch riders died, and last year three Belgians and two Dutch riders died.'[22]

Despite the lack of clear scientific evidence, the link between EPO becoming available and the unfortunate deaths of cyclists was repeated in media, policy and academic circles. In a way it made sense. A drug that was designed for patients with low red blood cell levels should not be given to those with normal blood levels. Moreover, it fitted with other accusations made against elite cyclists, including that doping was a normal part of the sport, that blood doping had been used for several years, and that cyclists sought out any potential ways to improve their performance. It also coincided with the growing awareness that cycling teams were consulting unscrupulous doctors such as Conconi and Michele Ferrari.

While outsiders lamented the corrupt nature of cycling, insiders closed ranks to establish a form of *omertà*, a self-policing culture of denial and secrecy. Very few cyclists broke this silence to expose doping and those who did (such as Paul Kimmage) were marginalized by other members of the cycling community. However, in the absence of a reliable test for exogenous EPO use, there was nothing to stop its spread among cyclists and other endurance sport athletes, despite it being widely perceived as a drug that could kill. Much like the Knud Enemark Jensen case in 1960, here was a convenient myth that anti-doping campaigners used to support their arguments for more testing and harsher punishments. Also, similarly to Jensen, a list of around twenty cyclists have been immortalized as having doped themselves to death, rather than them – and their families – being treated with sympathy and respect.

The scaremongering also meant that debates on how to develop policies were increasingly focused on absolutist ideas of complete abstinence. The voices of fear became stronger as doping was associated with East German abuses, steroids in the wider population, blood manipulation methods and substances that could be fatal and general mistrust of athletes and their medical support staff. The idea of a liberal or harm reduction approach, potentially allowing some performance-enhancing drugs to be taken within regulations, was crowded out by overenthusiastic hardliners. Some media reporting soaked up and regurgitated the fear-based narrative that far overshadowed any concerns for athletes' rights, disproportionate sanctions, the increasing complexities of prohibition that could trip up an innocent athlete, or indeed the fact that some athletes might end up doping through no choice of their own. The war on doping was gathering momentum at a cultural level if not yet at a policy level. It was supported by a general sense that sport was different to other drug contexts because athletes were obsessed with winning and doping presented an opportunity to do just that.

This jaundiced view of sport was epitomized by a feature in *Sports Illustrated* in 1997 that started:

> A scenario, from a 1995 poll of 198 sprinters, swimmers, powerlifters and other assorted athletes, most of them u.s. Olympians or aspiring Olympians: You are offered a banned performance-enhancing substance, with two guarantees: 1) You will not be caught. 2) You will win. Would you take the substance?
>
> One hundred and ninety-five athletes said yes; three said no.
>
> Scenario ii: You are offered a banned performance-enhancing substance that comes with two guarantees: 1) You will not be caught. 2) You will win every competition you enter for the next five years, and then you will die from the side effects of the substance. Would you take it?
>
> More than half the athletes said yes.[23]

The article went on to explain that this survey had been run every year since 1982 with similar results. It was bolstered by an opinion from an insider expert who supported the argument that doping was so rife that an aspiring athlete might have no choice but to resort to using performance-enhancing drugs:

> What is surprising is that 25 years after the introduction of supposedly rigorous drug testing of Olympic athletes, the use of banned performance-enhancing substances has apparently become more widespread, and effective, than ever. 'There may be some sportsmen who can win gold medals without taking drugs, but there are very few,' says Dutch physician Michel Karsten, who claims to have prescribed anabolic steroids to hundreds of world-class athletes from swimming, track and field and the non-Olympic sport of powerlifting over the

last 25 years. 'If you are especially gifted, you may win once, but from my experience you can't continue to win without drugs. The field is just too filled with drug users.'[24]

If such ideas dominated, they were based on individual opinions and in reference to surveys that were not conducted in a rigorous or scientific way, such as using peer-review and critical analysis. They offered a one-dimensional view of athletes as risk-takers and cheats, which cannot be generalized to all athletes. However, scandalous stories of underground maleficence, black-market suppliers and corrupt sports leaders intrigued readers and provoked debates about the effectiveness and value of anti-doping. Even within academic social science this debate seemed open enough to consider all sides of the argument. In 1996 David Black wrote for the *International Review for the Sociology of Sport* on the question: 'Does the Ban on Drugs in Sport Improve Societal Welfare?' To which, he proposed: 'Removal of the ban would result in an improvement in societal welfare by creating fairer sporting contests and reducing health risks facing athletes.' In 1997 Terry Black and Amelia Pape published an article in *Journal of Sport and Social Issues* that asked, 'The Ban on Drugs in Sport: The Solution or the Problem?' Two years later Verner Møller published a hugely controversial book in Danish, translated into English in 2007, called *The Doping Devil*. In this book Møller argued that the underpinning rationale for anti-doping is flawed and the problem was overstated. He then called for a reconsideration of the very foundations of the policies designed to control doping. This mirrored some critical studies a few years later that used the concept of 'moral panic' to analyse anti-doping. Certainly, there was scope around the late 1990s for a more open discussion about what doping meant, the value of anti-doping, the practicalities of anti-doping and engaging athletes in a more meaningful debate on these questions.

However, this debate largely never happened. Instead, a cycling scandal – closely related to the fears over EPO and blood doping risks – on the sport's biggest stage turned the tide for policy leaders, restricted the scope of academic discussions and undermined any suggestions for liberalization or harm reduction models.

The 1998 Tour de France Scandal

The use of blood doping, EPO, testosterone, painkillers, sleeping pills and stimulants – as well as party drugs – in the world of elite cycling would be exposed in the years 2008–12 as some of the most successful American teams fell apart and former teammates pointed fingers and confessed to their own roles in organized doping. However, in the 1990s few details had seeped out beyond the tight-knit inner circles engulfed by the code of silence. All of this would change in 1998 when a scandal centred initially upon Willy Voet, a physiotherapist for Festina, one of the top cycling teams in the world, broke just ahead of that year's Tour de France.

Festina was one of the most successful professional cycling teams in the 1990s. Among other titles, Festina won the team classification in the 1994 Tour de France and placed third in 1996 and second in 1997. The team's roster boasted some of the best cyclists in the world. One of Voet's jobs for the team was to look after their doping supplies. On 8 July 1998 he was stopped at the French–Belgian border while driving his team car. During a search, the police discovered extensive amounts of doping substances and paraphernalia. Along with syringes, they found EPO, steroids and stimulants. According to the press coverage at the time, this included '235 doses of erythropoietin (EPO), an artificial hormone which boosts the red cells (and therefore endurance) but can thicken the blood to fatal levels if not controlled properly. They also found 82 doses of a muscle-strengthening hormone called Sauratropine; 60 doses of Pantestone, a derivative of testosterone, which boosts body strength but can cause cancer; and sundry pain-deadening corticoids and energy-fuelling amphetamines.'[25]

Voet was arrested and the police began investigating Festina and several other leading teams. The Tour de France was scheduled to start on 11 July. The race became disorganized as some cyclists and teams withdrew, while others were investigated by police. The drama centred on hotel raids and arrests. Members of the Festina team were held in custody while being interviewed. The team was expelled by the Tour director and almost all of its members confessed to doping.

There was a sense of scandal and drama around this event, not least because it was unfolding during the race as more details emerged from Festina and other teams. An example of the reportage highlights the crisis:

On Friday, a revolt by riders occurred which delayed things for 2 hours. The flareup came after a report on France 2, showing a dustbin containing drugs used by certain participants. The riders claimed that this was a beat up and they were being treated as criminals. They said the media was more concerned with the doping instead of the race. But, isn't the race intrinsically tied up with the doping?

The influential French daily *Le Monde*, which on Friday called for the Tour to be stopped, published a confession from an anonymous professional rider today. The rider declared that his medical bills alone for drugs had cost around $A125,000 (or around $US100,000). The amount of 600,000 FF was quoted. The individual's doping was organised by the team. He said: 'There is not one team manager, team doctor, masseur, racing organiser who is not aware of the doping.' He backed up his claims with documents covering a daily dossier of a doctor.

The rider outlined the scheme of drug taking: three steroid tablets in the morning, and an injection of testosterone once a week. And regular EPO injections in increasing does until the maximum of 4,000 units is reached. And there were other forbidden substances taken including Human Growth Hormones. The regimen of drug taking was supervised by a private doctor.[26]

It was the high level of international publicity that made the events of 1998 so important. The investigations into Festina and another team caught with doping substances that year, TVM, went on for three more years. French politicians spoke openly about doping and the Tour organizers were under intense pressure to rid the sport of drug use. It became clear that doping was centrally managed by the teams rather than by the individual cyclists. Teams had doctors, and most had slush funds that took a percentage of prize money to pay for doping products and methods, as well as the expertise required to run them safely and undetected. It was also clear that the sport's governing body, the Union Cycliste Internationale (UCI), was not capable of preventing doping – much as the IOC had failed to prevent doping in the Olympics. These scandals highlighted the need for an agency that stood outside of the vested interests of each sport or country to run anti-doping. Due to international pressure on the IOC and sport in general, the IOC organized a conference to be held in its hometown – Lausanne, Switzerland – to explore the options for the future of global anti-doping.

The World Anti-Doping Agency

The conference held in January 1999 led to the Lausanne Declaration on Doping in Sport that set out a framework for an independent, global anti-doping organization. This was not in the ioc's original plan. The ioc fully expected to be the lead organization, even proposing that it be called the Olympic Anti-Doping Agency. However, the delegates at the conference voiced their criticisms of the ioc, saying it could not be trusted to lead this new approach. It was largely government ministers who noted concerns about sport being policed by an organization whose interests might conflict with anti-doping and called for a body with full independence from sport governing bodies and event organizers. The ioc president, Juan Antonio Samaranch, proposed that the ioc would accept the formation of a new body, so long as the ioc was integral to the organization. This compromise led to allowing the ioc to provide WADA with operating funds and the appointment of Dick Pound, an ioc vice president, as the first WADA president. After the conference, the ioc announced the new initiative:

> An independent International Anti-Doping Agency shall be established so as to be fully operational for the Games of the XXVII Olympiad in Sydney in 2000. This institution will have as its mandate, notably, to coordinate the various programmes necessary to realize the objectives that shall be defined jointly by all the parties concerned. Among these programmes, consideration should be given in particular to expanding out-of-competition testing, coordinating research, promoting preventive and educational actions and harmonizing scientific and technical standards and procedures for analyses and equipment. A working group representing the Olympic Movement, including the athletes, as well as the governments and inter-governmental organizations concerned, will meet, on the initiative of the ioc, within three months, to define the structure, mission and financing of the Agency. The Olympic Movement commits to allocate a capital of U.S. $25 million to the Agency.[27]

Dick Pound (right), first president of WADA, pictured in 2010 with Steven Ungerleider, author of *Faust's Gold* (2001).

As we explain in the next chapter, the strategies developed by WADA would revolutionize the nature of anti-doping and its impact on athletes. It had the full support of governments and inter-governmental agencies and organizations including the Council of Europe and UNESCO. The opportunity had passed for any real consideration of alternative approaches that might have included harm reduction models of drug use, specific policies for each sport or the pragmatic acceptance of the logic of performance enhancement. Instead, the world of sport focused on scandals, health fears, the abuse that might occur behind closed doors and the need for an improved image of sport to ensure public support for competitions and athletes as role models. The direction of travel has been neatly summarized by sociologist Ross Coomber:

a number of key drug myths and discursive positionings
. . . have emerged in the sporting world: for example, that
efficacious performance enhancement is a simple issue,
that the health risks are like playing Russian Roulette, that
doping undermines sport/morality to a degree that other
forms of cheating do not and that doping policy is rational
. . . a fear-based approach to drugs policy can result in a
policy that does not protect those it is supposed to and
results in a disproportionate and uninformed response.[28]

The new powers given to WADA would ultimately lead to such
consequences in the decades that followed. The 1990s, though, was
the decade during which anti-doping began its shift from being
a fragmented, disunited and disorganized system to one that was
increasingly centralized, standardized and bureaucratic. But like
many bureaucracies, the means would quickly become the end
in themselves, with the greater good sometimes forgotten in the
business of following the rules.

7

A New Approach

The events of November 1999 heralded a revolution in sport policymaking. For the first time, an organization existed that crossed both national boundaries and the silos of specific sports. Of course, this made sense. It would prevent athletes from suffering the consequences of varying rules, policy changes being made and not communicated well, confusion about whom they could appeal to and disparities in punishments depending on sport and country. It intended to force sport organizations to prioritize anti-doping and undercut the motivations and cultures that allowed doping to thrive. Most importantly, it aimed to prevent the sort of highly systematic regimes that existed in East Germany and potentially elsewhere. The vision was to make and keep sport free of doping for the sake of athletes' health, the protection of clean athletes and the integrity of sport.

The early 2000s, however, showed that the mechanisms for achieving these lofty goals would be controversial and problematic. When the World Anti-Doping Code (WADC) was first introduced in 2003, it set in motion a set of rules and procedures that blended soft power – a call to arms around the amorphous 'spirit of sport' ideal – and hard power as athletes who were caught breaking rules could face a ban regardless of the individual circumstances. Based on its monopoly of power, WADA introduced stringent rules and testing systems that improved detection and punishment but invaded athletes' privacy and punished innocuous violations. There was a price to be paid for 'clean sport'. WADA's new systems would increase surveillance and reveal cases of organized and individual doping, but it still struggled to rid sport of doping, cheating and deception.

More of the Same?

If the Cold War era of nationalist showboating in sport had come to an end, it was quickly replaced by other motivations for sporting success that encouraged doping. Money flowed into the Olympic movement, which did not pay athletes directly but allowed athletes to benefit from sponsorships, prize money and improved professional contracts with their governments or sports clubs. Outside of the Olympics, revolutions in media coverage and entrepreneurship boosted income for the main team sports, which to some extent trickled down into lower leagues and competitions. Prize money increased, as did players' wages in sports like football. Taken together, the conditions for doping remained fertile.

The decisions taken in Lausanne at the end of 1999 did not have an immediate impact on doping control. There was still very little out-of-competition anti-doping testing, leaving athletes who doped the opportunity to do so ahead of the Sydney Olympics. All they had to do was understand the 'wash-out' period and time their doping accordingly, use substances to mask steroid use such as diuretics or manipulate the Therapeutic Use Exemption system to get access to stimulants and painkillers. Another tactic of avoiding being caught was to swap urine samples. This could be done by hiding another sample in their clothing or bodies, or for men by using a prosthetic penis. More simply, they could avoid drug-control officers by not answering phone calls or the doorbell.

The science of drug testing lagged far behind the doping innovators. There were still no tests for blood doping, human growth hormone and other more complex pharmaceuticals. A reliable test for EPO was first introduced at the 2000 Olympic Games.[1] Despite this, there was some speculation that doping had remained a major issue in Sydney, as summarized in an article by *CBS News* in January 2002:

> Faster, higher and stronger, that's the Olympic ideal of pure competition between the world's best athletes. But what is the reality? According to some Olympic insiders, the summer games opening this week in Sydney Australia may be a competition between whose performance-enhancing drugs are better than the rest ... Drug testing for Olympic athletes is supposed to be the strictest it has ever been. The Sydney summer Games are supposed to be the 'cleanest' of any games. But what is the reality? Athletes and insiders say this is the 'dirtiest' summer Games ever, and that the International Olympic Committee (IOC) and the United States Olympic Committee (USOC) are in on the scam.[2]

This view was supported by some survey evidence, supposedly conducted by the White House, although no further details were given. The article went on: 'Just how prevalent is the use of performance-enhancing drugs by Olympic athletes? According to the International Olympic Committee (IOC), it's a tiny percentage. According to a $1 million White House study ... in some sports it's closer to 90 percent.'[3] Again, unreliable data was seized upon to create a narrative of very high levels of doping.

The official drug-testing statistics for the first set of Olympic Games of the new millennium showed nothing too troubling. Thirteen athletes tested positive during the 2000 Games in Sydney, which seems like a trivial number considering there were 10,651 athletes competing. One of those cases, that of the sixteen-year-old Romanian gymnast Andreea Răducan, was problematic in that she was stripped of her gold medal merely for following the advice of her team doctor, who supplied her with medication to reduce the symptoms of a common cold. She was given Nurofen that contained pseudoephedrine. She was exonerated on appeal of the decision, but the IOC refused to return her medal. In what now seems like a draconian consequence, the team doctor was expelled from the 2000 Games and banned from having a role in the 2004 and 2008 Games. Ion Ţiriac, head of the Romanian Olympic Committee, also resigned from his position. Ţiriac was defiant in his criticism of the decisions, highlighting the disparity of resources – the team doctor was not a sports specialist, he worked in a small hospital and volunteered for the Olympics role. The IOC and the arbitrators admitted the athlete had done nothing wrong, but they felt obliged to impose the rules. Ţiriac said, 'The IOC is between a rock and a hard place. They are under political pressure [on doping] but they do not have the courage to say that in this case they have made a mistake. There must be leniency . . . innocent people should not be punished.'[4]

Speculation about doping was boosted by the Australian shot putter Werner Reiterer, who published a book in 2000 that detailed the popularity of steroid use, especially in strength sports, and the lack of concern shown by coaches, doctors and sports leaders. He also claimed that it was easy to beat the tests:

> He worked with a doctor designing the usual menu of steroids and masking agents and growth hormones. He found that by a quirk of his physiology his testosterone level seemed unable to rise above a ratio of 3:1 with his epitestosterone. The IOC limit is 6:1 and the IOC can't even test for growth hormones. Plain sailing.[5]

A similar situation occurred in professional cycling. On the face of it, the Festina scandal should have ushered in a greater concern for preventive anti-doping measures and more awareness among the cyclists of the risks of being caught. The 1999 Tour de France was won by Lance Armstrong, who would subsequently lose that title more than a decade later for doping. Many of the other top-placed riders that year had been part of doping scandals, and two of the main Festina riders from the 1998 scandal were among them: Alex Zülle, who finished second, and Richard Virenque, who was eighth. Armstrong also found success in both the 2000 Tour de France and the 2000 Olympics, in which he won a bronze medal that would be taken from him later.

The Winter Olympic Games in 2002 had ten positive doping cases. This was a substantial increase for winter sports, as there had been no positives for doping at a Winter Olympics since 1988, when there was one. Four of the 2002 cases were associated with the Austrian team, which had some members engaging in blood doping with the support of team officials. This incident did not prevent the Austrians from becoming involved in a scandal during the 2006 Games, when Italian police raided their rooms and found doping substances, leading to six athletes being banned for life.[6]

One of the cases in 2002 once again illustrated the potential risks of an overly strict interpretation of anti-doping coupled with inconsistent decision-making processes. The Scottish skier Alain Baxter had achieved something that very few Brits had previously – a medal at the Winter Olympics. After his bronze position in the downhill slalom made him the first British athlete to win a medal in skiing, he tested positive for levomethamphetamine. It was agreed by officials that this substance had no significant performance-enhancing properties, and Baxter proved it came from his use of the American version of a Vicks-brand nasal inhaler. The UK version Baxter normally used did not contain levomethamphetamine and he did not expect there to be any difference between the two products. Nonetheless, he was disqualified and stripped of his medal. The International Ski Federation banned him for

Rio Ferdinand (right), footballer for Manchester United, who was banned in 2003–4 for missing a test, pictured here in 2009.

three months, though this was overturned on appeal. Even though he was not sanctioned beyond the Olympics, the IOC refused to change its decision. Baxter continued as a competitive skier but was never able to replicate his (short-lived) Olympic success.

Another case that tested the legal processes ahead of the new WADC taking effect was that of footballer Rio Ferdinand, who played for Manchester United and the England national team. An anti-doping test officer arrived at the club's training ground and requested that Ferdinand be available for testing. He had already left and had turned off his mobile phone. The decision to ban him for eight months took three months of deliberations and teams of expensive lawyers, and his sanction remained controversial. England's manager, Sven-Göran Eriksson, wanted it to be shorter as the European Championships were to be held in summer 2004. It also came to light that a similar case involving the Manchester City player Christian Negouai had resulted in a fine rather than a ban. As football's world governing body, FIFA, had yet to become a signatory to the WADC, the decision was left to the English FA with FIFA president Sepp Blatter insisting on a sanction for the player.[7] Ferdinand missed the European Championships but returned to both club and country for the 2004–5 season.

The 2003 World Anti-Doping Code

The years between the Festina scandal and the publication of the first version of the Code were characterized by two contesting themes: ongoing problems with systematic and individual doping to cheat on one side, and innocuous cases with unclear decision-making processes on the other. The WADC was designed to fulfil several functions, with the primary one being to prevent doping through testing, education and the fear of punishment. However, testing would need to be improved as it was clear that a large number of athletes felt able to avoid being caught, while education was designed to discourage doping before it occurred. Punishments were ramped up to show how serious the global sports community was about stamping out doping.

To achieve these lofty ambitions, WADA needed to persuade countries and sports to sign up to the new Code. This standardization was, at the same time, a handover of power. There was no option for individual athletes to buy into some of the WADC, and refusal by countries or sports federations to become a signatory was seen as not taking doping seriously. WADA's was a rigid system from the beginning, leaving little space for resistance, negotiation, flexibility or consideration of specific circumstances. As cases and decisions had previously highlighted, an appeals process was needed to improve consistency. WADA used the Court of Arbitration for Sport (CAS), which had been set up by the IOC in 1984.

The central pillar of WADA and its Code was the creation of a 'List of Prohibited Substances and Methods', accompanied by a stated rationale for deciding why a substance or method should be banned. WADA gave three criteria for determining if a substance or method made it onto the list, and any substance or method had to meet only two of them. First, it needed to present a risk or potential risk to the health of the athlete. Second, a substance or method needed to be performance-enhancing or potentially performance-enhancing. Third was that it contravened the vaguely defined notion of the 'spirit of sport'. A substance is usually a drug, traces of which would usually be found in athletes' urine samples. WADA confirmed the 'strict liability' rule, which the IOC had already introduced, which held that the athlete was deemed responsible for any substance found in their sample and should be punished accordingly. Punishments were set out as bans from sport. The 2003 Code stated that substances in the categories with the most performance-enhancement benefits – anabolic steroids and peptide hormones – would lead to a two-year ban from all sport. Other substances would have a reduced sanction.

The criteria used are controversial. As noted already, there was a tendency among anti-doping leaders and media reporters to assume the worst of substances and overstate the risks of their use. Many substances on the prohibited list had not been researched in detail regarding the potential range of health risks. Further, substances that were considered to be performance-enhancing might not actually have had a huge impact on an athlete's abilities, especially in team sports, skill-based sports or cognitive sports such as bridge or chess. However, the even fuzzier notion is the 'spirit of sport'. This was first developed in Canada in the aftermath of the Dubin Inquiry as a way to reinforce the positive values for all participants in sport. The definition provided in the WADC also highlights the influence of the IOC on WADA:

> Anti-doping programs seek to preserve what is intrinsically valuable about sport. This intrinsic value is often referred

to as 'the spirit of sport'. It is the essence of Olympism, the pursuit of human excellence through the dedicated perfection of each person's talents. It is how we play true. The spirit of sport is the celebration of the human spirit, body and mind, and is reflected in values we find in and through sport, including Ethics, fair play and honesty; health; excellence in performance; character and education; fun and joy; teamwork; dedication and commitment; respect for rules and laws; respect for self and other Participants; courage; community and solidarity.[8]

The mention of 'methods' of doping referred primarily to blood doping but also to the prospect of gene doping, even though there was no test for the latter or evidence of its use. The focal point was the urine sample, to discover what WADA calls 'analytical evidence', leading to the term 'adverse analytical finding' to describe a positive test. Given the importance of the urine sample, WADA also introduced a set of procedures for ensuring that the sample could not be swapped or tampered with. Indeed, one of the anti-doping rule violations (ADRV) is for tampering – which means an athlete or a team member could be banned from sport if they do not follow the strict protocols for providing a sample. Avoiding a test is another type of ADRV.

The consequences of these policies and procedures impacted heavily upon clean athletes as much as it did the cheats. If the urine sample was to be guaranteed to be that of the athlete, the drug control officer (DCO) had to observe the urine leaving their body. The DCO would need to chaperone the athlete from the point of notification until they were ready to urinate. They would then follow the athlete to the bathroom, insist they stripped from the waist to expose their genitals, and observe the delivery of the urine into a sample bottle that was then split into two bottles in case a second test was required.

In order to prevent doping done outside the time surrounding a competition where testing would be conducted, WADA introduced a more rigorous system of out-of-competition testing. Under this approach, athletes could be notified of a test any day, at any time and in any place, including their home, on holiday or anywhere they were located by a tester. If they refused, they would receive a two-year ban. Some athletes would also be selected for the Registered Testing Pool (RTP). These athletes had to provide anti-doping agencies with information about where they could be found for one hour every day so they could be reached by drug testers. This type of 24-hour availability and surveillance is usually reserved for groups such as convicted criminals. Athletes are not permitted time off from the threat of testing for the entirety of the time they are in the RTP.

Another way athletes' privacy was compromised was through having to list all the medicines or drugs they were using even if they were not banned, ostensibly to avoid any potential confusion when the sample was analysed. This disclosure risked revealing aspects of an athlete's medical history or conditions to anti-doping agencies. However, this was an effort to further ensure that athletes were solely responsible in the event of a positive test for a prohibited substance. Failing to disclose a medication or supplement may undermine an athlete's defence, so the requirement to provide these also functioned as a way of bolstering strict liability. This, in turn, could either prevent appeals of positive tests or be used as evidence that an athlete was trying to cover up their use.

Strict liability was a potentially tough sell outside of sport, meaning athlete appeals through national court systems could potentially undermine WADA's enforcement of the rule. WADA's solution to the problems of appeals being taken to non-sports courts was to ensure that the only course of appeal was through a tribunal held by the athlete's National Anti-Doping Organisation or by the Court of Arbitration for Sport. By doing so, decisions on sanctions would be made by sports federations in accordance with the wadc. Any appeal could only be made on procedural grounds and directly in relation to the wadc Articles. Given the strict liability rule, appeals relating to lack of intent or contamination were very rarely successful and, even if they were successful, would usually lead only to a reduced ban rather than a complete exoneration.

These policies were developed in a hurry, in response to the sense of crisis among sports leaders and governments that had been given a focal point at the Lausanne conference. They were also created with very little consultation with the very people who would be most affected: athletes. At the time, it may well have looked as if wada was making progress in the war on doping, cracking down on cheating through detection and sanctions, and developing a structure of prevention with its education initiatives. It appeared to be independent, and recommended that all countries or regions create an independent anti-doping organization. wada's leaders sought political support and funding from governments, and in 2007 the wadc was bolstered by a unesco convention that governments could sign onto in support of the fight for clean sport. wada then had support from the highest level of politics and international sports. wada also had a monopoly of power over how to develop testing and the rules around anti-doping. For example, in 2009 the ban for performance-enhancing drug use was extended to four years for a first offence.

Successes

Doping became more of an issue in the 2004 Summer Olympic Games. It began with a national scandal for the host country, involving two high-profile Greek sprinters, Costas Kenteris and Katerina Thanou. Both were medal hopefuls in their events following a successful Games in 2000. Kenteris had won the 200-metre gold in Sydney, and Thanou took silver in the 100 metres. As a result of his success representing Greece, Kenteris was scheduled to light the Olympic flame at the opening ceremony. However, the pair had been identified for anti-doping testing but were not at the athletes' village. The case became worldwide news when photographs showed them in hospital following being injured in a motorcycle accident. They claimed that the accident occurred as they rushed back to the Olympic village. Due to conflicting accounts, there was suspicion that they had faked the crash to avoid being drug tested. It was reported that:

> They then spent four days in hospital before facing an International Olympic Committee (IOC) disciplinary panel that urged them to withdraw amid a global whirlwind of publicity . . . The number of differing accounts from people including team officials and Hellenic Olympic Committee officials quickly eroded support for the athletes and their coach, all of whom faced additional charges of staging the accident and filing false reports to police.[9]

While the truth of the incident remains unclear, the disputes continued for two years before the athletes admitted using performance-enhancing drugs and were banned from sport for two years. The Greek athletics federation blamed the athletes, but it did ban their coach for four years. Following this scandal, Kenteris did not compete again, and while Thanou did return to competition, her career was never as successful.

Investigations into doping in U.S. sport were beginning to show that it remained an issue at the highest levels of sport. A new form of steroid, tetrahydrogestrinone or THG, was produced by Patrick Arnold and Victor Conte at the Bay Area Laboratory Co-operative (BALCO). THG, also known as 'the clear', was undetectable to anti-doping tests and Conte designed a range of further strategies to prevent athletes being caught. Several high-profile athletes were found guilty of doping across a range of sports, including baseball, American football and athletics. The doping system was discovered after whistleblower evidence was sent to the United States Anti-Doping Agency by disgruntled coach Trevor Graham in the form of a syringe containing THG. One of Graham's athletes, multiple Olympic and World Championship gold medallist Marion Jones, was later found guilty of cheque fraud related to her involvement with BALCO and served six months in federal prison.

The fallout from BALCO was a national scandal, especially as it implicated athletes from U.S. professional sports, most notably baseball. It even led to President George W. Bush discussing the issue in his 2004 State of the Union address:

> To help children make right choices, they need good examples. Athletics play such an important role in our society, but, unfortunately, some in professional sports are not setting much of an example. The use of performance-enhancing drugs like steroids in baseball, football, and other sports is dangerous, and it sends the wrong message – that there are shortcuts to accomplishment, and that performance is more important than character. So tonight I call on team owners, union representatives, coaches and players to take the lead, to send the right signal, to get tough, and to get rid of steroids now.[10]

This call echoed what WADA was trying to initiate within Olympic sport. Bush's call for tougher anti-doping was followed by the passage of the 2004 Anabolic Steroid Control Act, which expanded what could be included, and therefore regulated, as an anabolic steroid.

Systematic Doping Continues

One unintended consequence of the upscaled war on doping was to make organized doping more sophisticated. Once WADA-accredited laboratories could test for smaller traces of substances and out-of-competition testing became more frequent, the traditional wash-out period approach of avoiding detection was derailed. This meant that novel strategies for beating the tests were required. The scientists supporting WADA developed a new method that focused on monitoring blood levels over a period of months and years to find and assess variations among specific markers that might indicate doping. This Athlete Biological Passport (ABP) was introduced in 2008. Once the ABP and new tests were introduced for human growth hormone, EPO and blood doping, a more determined method was required to get the same benefits. The BALCO case was indicative of continued determination to beat the testers. They used new drugs unknown to anti-doping regulators, such as THG, and those for which there was no test, such as insulin. Victor Conte instructed athletes on how to avoid the testers by not responding to phone calls and lying about their whereabouts. Under WADA's rules, athletes could miss one test without a penalty.

The experience of English sprinter Dwain Chambers highlights how athletes could get drawn into such a system. He was disappointed with a string of race performances and heard about BALCO. Conte told him that he needed more performanceenhancing drugs and assured him that he would not be caught. Chambers was only identified for an out-of-competition test after Trevor Graham's evidence led to a wide-ranging investigation. Chambers was banned for two years as a result. In the aftermath of his sanction, Conte wrote a letter to him explaining the drugs he was given and the procedures involved. Chambers wrote in his autobiography that he did not understand doping or the WADC 'List of Prohibited

Substances and Methods'. He needed the support of experts like Conte and Patrick Arnold:

Your performance enhancing drug program included the following seven prohibited substances: THG, testosterone/ epitestosterone cream, EPO (Procrit), HGH (Serostim), insulin (Humalog), modafinil (Provigil) and liothryonine, which is a synthetic form of the T3 thyroid hormone (Cytomel).[11]

In his letter to Chambers, Conte detailed how each substance was used and for which purposes, as well as the rough schedule for when each would be most effective during both competition and off-season times. The letter also explained how so many athletes had been able to beat out-of-competition anti-doping testing. This main method was simply avoiding testers using various excuses until a substance would no longer be detectable. This included strategically missing a test if a positive result was likely, which was and still is allowed under anti-doping rules.

International athletics was plagued by doping during this time, the evidence of which, however, would not be revealed until 2015 following investigation into stored samples and analysis records. While the ABP protocols and regulations were still under development, the IAAF collected blood samples from over 5,000 athletes in 208 countries between 2002 and 2011. These showed very high levels of suspicious blood values, which likely could only have been increased using artificial methods such as EPO or blood doping. The *Sunday Times* coverage summarized the findings:

A third of all medals in endurance events at the world championships and Olympics, including 55 gold medals, were won by athletes who had given suspicious blood samples at some point in their careers.

Ten medals awarded at the London Olympics were won by athletes who have had suspicious blood test results.

More than 80% of Russia's Olympic and world championship medals were won by suspicious athletes.

Kenya is renowned for producing many of the world's greatest distance runners but 18 of the country's medals were won by athletes judged to have had suspicious blood test results.[12]

When analysed by country, the findings showed doping was indeed a global problem. The results showed that large proportions of some countries' athletes were returning suspicious values, including Russia (30 per cent), Ukraine (28 per cent), Turkey (27 per cent), Greece (26 per cent), Morocco (24 per cent), Bulgaria (22 per cent), Bahrain (20 per cent), Belarus (19 per cent), Slovenia (16 per cent), Romania (13 per cent), Brazil (12 per cent) and a host of other countries with slightly lower results. That so many athletes had seemingly gotten away with doping despite all the testing developments, strict policies and harsh sanctions called into question the veracity of the anti-doping system's claims about rooting out doping.

The extent of this doping has been exposed in other ways as well. A survey of athletes at two international track and field events in 2011 provided further evidence of what was happening in that sport. The researchers surveyed 2,167 athletes at two athletics events: the thirteenth International Association of Athletics Federations World Championships (wca) in Daegu, South Korea, in August 2011, and the twelfth Quadrennial Pan-Arab Games (pag) in Doha, Qatar, in December 2011. Using the randomized-response technique that models prevalence based on responses to questions using a randomizing tool – intended to provide greater assurance of anonymity and reduce the risk of socially biased responses – the survey found that 44 per cent of athletes admitted using doping substances or methods in the previous twelve months.[13]

The scale of this doping also affected the 2012 Olympic Games in London. During the event only nine athletes tested positive. However, over 5,000 samples provided during that time have since been retested on the basis of new evidence of doping stemming from the Russian scandal, which we will consider in a moment, and new testing methods. By the end of the eight-year statute of limitations (raised to ten years in the 2015 WADC), 139 athletes from the 2012 Games had been found guilty of doping and punished through disqualification and bans. This is a significant increase from the 2008 Olympics, at which 81 athletes were disqualified or banned. Both are far in excess of the number of positive anti-doping tests at any Games before WADA was empowered to conduct retrospective investigations and re-test samples after an event had finished. For the 2012 Olympics, the total number of athletes found to have doped includes 39 medallists, of whom thirteen had won gold medals. Russia had the most doping cases (46), followed by Ukraine (seventeen), Belarus (fifteen) and Turkey (fourteen). The sports with the highest numbers of athletes testing positive were athletics (91) and weightlifting (34).[14] The legacy of London 2012, which had billed itself as the cleanest Olympics ever, was completely undermined by the revelations of the huge number of athletes and medallists who had been doping undetected during the Games. Given the successes of the re-testing, the statute of limitations was increased to ten years for samples taken in 2015 onwards.

Cycling: Systematic Doping to Reform

When Lance Armstrong won his record-breaking seventh Tour de France title in 2005, he made the following comments: 'I'll say to the people who don't believe, the cynics and the sceptics: I'm sorry for you. I'm sorry you don't believe in miracles.'[15] When he retired it did look as if the doping accusations made against him

Lance Armstrong (left) and team manager Johan Bruyneel, pictured in 2009 during Armstrong's comeback season.

would disappear since there was no positive test or other analytical evidence to show that he had doped during his career. In short, he had not been caught.

The step-by-step details of how his downfall occurred have been well covered in books, documentaries, interviews and articles. He famously confessed to doping in a prime-time interview with Oprah Winfrey. There were many key moments that precipitated his fall from grace. Instead of retiring, he returned to the sport in 2008, putting himself back in the spotlight but also creating conflict with his former teammate Floyd Landis, who had tested positive for elevated testosterone after winning the 2006 Tour de France. When details of the doping programme began to surface from those with first-hand experience of Armstrong's doping, including Landis, Tyler Hamilton, George Hincapie, Frankie Andreu and former masseuse Emma O'Reilly, USADA had sufficient evidence to publish a report in 2012 on the team doping system led by Armstrong. This report built on investigations by the FBI and the work of journalists David Walsh and Pierre Ballester.

The teams Armstrong led built their doping programmes on the advice of two doctors, the most important being Michele Ferrari. Much of the evidence presented linked Armstrong to the doctor, including visits to his clinic and transfers of payments. Ferrari was banned from sport for life. It was clear that not much had changed since the Festina scandal, except an increase in caution about transporting the drugs and avoiding out-of-competition testing. This was also the first case for which a sanction was delivered based on non-analytical evidence.

The highly organized nature of doping had also been discovered in May 2006 when Spanish police raided the clinic of Eufemiano Fuentes. This investigation into Fuentes's clinic and practice emerged from the testimony provided by cyclist Jesús Manzano in 2004. This information related directly to the Kelme team for which Fuentes had acted as a team doctor. As was reported: 'in an apartment belonging to Fuentes, approximately a thousand doses of anabolic steroids and hormones were seized, along with two hundred packets of blood, products to manipulate

Floyd Landis (centre), Tour de France, 2006.

Fans protest at the Tour de France, 2006.

it, machines to freeze it and material to perform transfusions.'[16] However, others were involved and the Spanish police made several arrests. Some leading cyclists eventually admitted being doped by Fuentes, but many others who were suspected were not sanctioned owing to a lack of evidence. Fuentes also claimed to have worked with international football and tennis players, though no further investigations have been undertaken on these due to problems with legal jurisdiction. In 2013 a Spanish court ruled that blood bags containing evidence of doping should be destroyed. After lengthy court battles, WADA received permission to analyse 215 seized blood bags. However, this did not come to the conclusion that anti-doping authorities were hoping for:

> More delays followed before WADA was able to access and analyse samples from athletes suspected of being part of the ring with DNA from the blood bags. WADA said it concluded the Puerto investigation in August. 'In total, 11 athletes (10 male and one female) have been identified through

this process as clients of Dr Fuentes,' WADA confirmed in its annual report. 'However, due to the 10-year statute of limitations having elapsed, names can no longer be made public.' Current world champion Alejandro Valverde is the only cyclist who received a ban as a result of Operation Puerto to still be racing at the highest level – the 39-year-old finished second at the recent *Vuelta a Espana*.[17]

In the aftermath of these cases, professional cycling has managed to avoid any scandals of a similar magnitude. Certainly, the imposition of WADA regulations and more determined investigations helped to crack down on doping doctors and systematic cheating. The ABP also offered testers an additional weapon to pursue cases, as did the push for whistle-blowers to come forward. The sport's governing body, the UCI, took a more focused approach to anti-doping as well. It had been stung by accusations that its leadership had passively allowed Lance Armstrong and his teammates, and of course other teams who were also engaging in doping to some extent, to continue the sort of doping systems that had been exposed in the late 1990s.[18] Several teams had a proactive approach to anti-doping, and some collectively established the Movement for Credible Cycling. Team Sky, based in the UK, did not join this organization, but established internal rules that it would not employ any cyclist or coach who had previously been caught doping. During the mid-2010s it faced accusations of doping, though not of the same scale as in previous cases. The most famous was the excess salbutamol that Chris Froome tested positive for, related to his asthma inhaler. He was banned for seven months, but was eventually cleared nine months after his positive test.

The Russia Crisis

After a decade and a half of relative success, the greatest challenge that WADA had to confront was the systematic doping of Russian athletes that occurred from the mid-2000s until 2016, when it was exposed by various investigations and the documentary *Icarus*. There remains some dispute about how many athletes took part in this system. In his report for WADA, Richard McLaren said that more than a thousand athletes had 'benefitted' from the programme, a comment that gained international media attention.[19] The key players at the centre of the conspiracy also created controversy as the former head of Russia's anti-doping laboratory Grigory Rodchenkov went into hiding in the USA fearing for his life. Russia was sanctioned with official exclusion from many international sport events and the Olympics, though some athletes were able to compete independently in the latter. Russia's WADA-accredited laboratory had been central to the cover-up, using various methods of subterfuge to hide positive doping results. It was also alleged that the Russian secret police service had assisted in the doping programme, especially when Russia hosted the 2014 Winter Olympics in Sochi. Among the many revelations was that the Russians had found a way of opening what were believed to be tamper-proof sample bottles, replacing the contents and then resealing them, without any other party suspecting malpractice. There was also an elaborate sample-swapping operation that included exchanging sample bottles through a hole in the wall into a shadow laboratory to avoid detection by observers.

The legal and political aftermath has been fraught with arguments and claims of vested interests. Some have argued that the doping programme was extensive and that almost all Russian athletes were forced to participate. However, the legal processes instigated by Russian athletes to clear their names led to many of them being excluded from blanket competition bans. Some high-profile athletes claimed they were disappointed that more sanctions were not imposed on Russia. The Canadian athlete Beckie Scott, chair of the WADA Athlete Committee, said she wanted Russia banned from the Olympics as it 'made a mockery of not only those who play by the rules, but those who create and safeguard them'.[20]

The Russia scandal mirrored the events of East Germany in the 1980s and '90s, and the speculation about Soviet-era doping programmes. It was precisely the sort of situation that WADA was created to prevent. It showed that a well-planned doping regime could still exist under WADA's watchful gaze if the right people were part of the corruption. There is no question that WADA cannot be in all countries at all times – it cannot enforce its own rules, and relies on local leaders, doctors, scientists and others to support anti-doping and not to undermine it. It seems the stakes of global sport are too high for some not to be tempted.

Of course, the irony is that Russia was getting away with its large-scale doping programme while other athletes were suffering from the extensive and unforgiving nature of the WADC. They continued to endure the humiliation of urine tests, surveillance through the out-of-competition testing rules, disproportionate punishments for minor offences and inadvertent positive cases from contamination or lack of education. These issues increasingly affected amateur athletes. The Russia scandal showed that the justification for such draconian measures was a myth – sport could not be cleaned up through more testing and harsher sanctions. While some have argued that the scandal should lead to tougher punishments, especially for ringleaders and countries that harbour them, our next chapter explores how WADA's approach unfairly impacts athletes and proposes that policies can be improved in ways that support athletes, who need to be consulted and engaged with rather than treated like criminal suspects.

8

Problems and Proposals

Sport has seen significant change and development in recent decades, including in the ways it is contested, consumed and presented in global media. Anti-doping is no exception. The continuing pattern of change since the 1960s has been the increasing power of anti-doping authorities to monitor and punish athletes for doping violations and infractions. The attempt to achieve clean sport under WADA is based on an uneasy blend of persuasion, prevention, fear and bans from competition. WADA's authority has extended beyond athletes to include their support personnel, which in some cases includes athletes' parents. The reach of monitoring and punishment has also extended beyond elite athletes to recreational and age-group competitors. The 'List of Banned Substances and Methods' has grown, while scientific analyses have become more adept at finding minuscule traces of banned substances or temporary fluctuations in blood values that are assumed to be caused by doping. Sanctions have been increased to four years for a first offence, and appeals are often out of the reach of less wealthy athletes. Even with financial resources, appeals are unlikely to succeed.

However, it is unclear whether the empowerment of antidoping has been effective at delivering clean sport since there are no reliable prevalence studies, and while hundreds of athletes each year are found guilty of doping, the authorities are no doubt missing out on many athletes across age and competitive levels who use performance-enhancing drugs. Indeed, the cases of the past twenty years show the continued willingness of sports organizations and some athletes to break the rules. There is understandably a degree of scepticism among athletes and other stakeholders, including fans, about how successful this global policy really is.

In parallel with the increased reach of WADA, there have also been problems with how athletes are treated in the anti-doping system. There are clear cases of over-zealous decisions leading to punishments that have severely damaged athletes' careers and well-being. There have been several cases of suicide or attempted suicide possibly linked to sanctioned athletes' struggles to cope with the public humiliation and loss of career prospects.

In this chapter, we assess the ineffectiveness of anti-doping, present case study examples of athletes who have been disproportionately punished and then provide some proposals to address these apparently intractable problems. We explore how to get to a situation where anti-doping can function in a more reasonable and humane way, based on a more appropriate sense of what 'clean sport' could look like and how it could be put into practice. While we make several suggestions, our principal idea is that athletes should be consulted, listened to, respected and encouraged to share their views on what type of policy they want and how to achieve it. After all, sport is nothing without athletes, and anti-doping has always purported to be in the athletes' best interests. The development of a top-down model of governance has led to athletes being disempowered. We propose a more open and democratic engagement with athletes across the competitive spectrum. First, though, we need to consider the ambivalent nature of the current situation.

The Ineffectiveness of Anti-Doping

In 2019, twenty years after the Lausanne conference that led to WADA's creation, two leading scholars in the field of social science anti-doping research, Ivan Waddington and Verner Møller, wrote:

> WADA's policies represent a missed opportunity for, far from bringing new thinking or offering a new approach to anti-doping, WADA has for the most part simply reiterated and intensified policies which have a long history of failure and [which] continue to be largely unsuccessful in controlling drug use in sport.[1]

The scale of doping represented by the cases detailed in previous chapters shows that doping has continued despite the development of a global framework for education, testing and sanctions by WADA. This is especially true of systematic doping. The scandals of recent decades are only the known cases of organized doping: the most successful systems are the ones we are not aware of. It would only take a complicit set of leaders to help organize and support a high-level doping system. WADA does not have the resources or authority to investigate every country and is largely dependent on the local anti-doping organization to monitor and flag any potential doping operations. We know that corruption has persisted in many sectors of sport, especially around financial opportunities, and that anti-doping rules can be easily subverted.

A prime example of this is Romania. As covered by The Sports Integrity Initiative, a report by WADA showed that the national anti-doping agency (ANAD) directed the Bucharest Laboratory to cover up positive doping tests relating to at least three athletes. This corruption was endemic:

The directions were given by Dr Graziela Elena Vâjialǎ, President of ANAD from its foundation in 2005 until January 2019, when she was replaced by Pavel-Christian Balaj after retiring from office 'on request', as ANAD puts it. The Report also found that Valentina Alexandrescu, Director General of ANAD, 'was, at best, wilfully blind to the misconduct of President Vajiala or, at worst, actively complicit'. It also appears that Alexandrescu was still employed by ANAD on 14 May, after Balaj took over from Vâjialǎ as ANAD President. WADA's Report, presented as Agenda Item #12.4 at its 16 May Foundation Board meeting, recommends that both are dismissed from their posts.

The Sports Integrity Initiative received the report from a whistleblower, and explained:

> It builds on an earlier November 2017 Report, which found that former Director and Deputy Director of the Laboratory, Valentin Pop and Mirela Zorio, were directed to cover up two adverse analytical findings (AAFs) by a third party. It identifies that third party as ANAD, under the direction of Vâjialǎ.[2]

One central paradox of anti-doping – and the key reason for the critical approach we have taken – is that WADA and its stakeholders place almost no trust in athletes, subject them to various forms of invasive surveillance and punish even the most minor discretions, but simultaneously assume that sports organization leaders, directors of laboratories and drug-control officers can all be trusted to take their responsibilities seriously and follow the rules. The Russia scandal showed that senior sport and anti-doping personnel can work together to manipulate the anti-doping system, especially when supported by politicians and police in their country.

This scale of such corruption has also been uncovered within sports federations. The IAAF president from 1999 to 2015, Lamine Diack, was directly involved in covering up doping cases and accepted bribes to do so. In 2020 it was revealed that he created a scheme in which athletes paid to have their doping positives disappear, for what he called 'full protection'. In other words, the very person whose job it was to help ensure athletics was drug-free had a well-organized system tantamount to blackmail that actively promoted a doping culture by allowing dopers to compete in major events.

One athlete caught up in this web of deceit was the Russian marathon runner Liliya Shobukhova. An investigation into her found she had paid senior figures in the IAAF €450,000 to cover up evidence of doping ahead of the 2012 Olympics. Following her ban in 2014 Shobukhova eventually turned whistle-blower in the investigation and implicated high-level IAAF officials who reportedly offered her protection from a doping ban. In total, investigators discovered 22 other Russian athletes had paid for the same service, with the amounts ranging from €100,000 to €600,000 and totalling €3.2 million. These athletes were effectively paying to cover up evidence of doping so they could compete at the Olympics in 2012 and World Championships in Moscow a year later. To support this corruption, Diack and his son Papa Massata Diack paid €200,000 to Gabriel Dollé, the former director of the IAAF's medical and anti-doping department. Again, the very individual responsible for directly managing anti-doping was in fact undermining it. The corruption within the organization was broader and included Diack's son at the very centre. It was reported that up to €15 million of diverted funds were involved. The judge in Lamine Diack's criminal case summed up the situation in 2020:

After sentencing Diack Sr to four years in prison – two of which are suspended – and fining him €500,000, the

judge, Rose-Marie Hunault, told the court in Paris: 'The
€3.2m was paid in exchange for a program of "full protection",' adding the scheme allowed athletes who should have
been suspended 'purely and simply to escape sanctions. You
violated the rules of the game.'[3]

Other types of evidence appear to show how WADA's testing
processes are not effective. Social science surveys using the ran-
domized response technique (designed to give respondents the
assurance of confidentiality) have collectively shown that doping
prevalence is much higher than the approximately 1.5 per cent rou-
tinely shown in WADA's Annual Testing Statistics. Survey results
have ranged from around 3 per cent to 40 per cent depending
on the sport and country. These results might be inflated by the
questions asked, which are mostly broad questions about whether
they have used a banned substance in the previous twelve months
or ever in their lifetime. Nonetheless, there are consistent survey
results reporting troubling levels of likely doping prevalence.[4]

If there is such a significant disparity in the WADA numbers
and true levels of doping, the implications are profound: many
athletes are doping and getting away with it. There are some potential reasons for this. Athletes might have used a doping drug or
method and simply not been tested in the period during which
it could be discovered. They might have done this in a planned
way that included strategizing how to avoid being tested when
they were likely to test positive. If so, they are intelligently out-
witting the testers. Or they might live in a country where very
little out-of-competition testing takes place. Testing is expensive
– around £800 per test – which means some countries do not
fund a comprehensive programme. Or it is possible that a specific country or sport does not want to expose doping, especially
among its top athletes, and so operates a testing system focused
on less-well-known athletes. Alternatively, the testers might focus

on the build-up to international events to show how 'clean' these are, which athletes could likely predict and therefore move their doping up so that it would take place earlier in the training season. Regardless of the reasons, it is clear that anti-doping strategies of education, testing and sanctions are not enough to prevent athletes and their support staff from breaking the rules.

COVID-19 and Anti-Doping

The challenges of delivering a testing programme that acts as an effective deterrent and catches dopers were exacerbated in 2020–21 by the impact of the COVID-19 pandemic. A WADA survey in 2020 found that 91 anti-doping organizations had stopped testing completely. An example is the UK, where testing fell from 2,017 for a three-month period in 2019 to just 124 for the same period in 2020. Regarding specific sports, tennis is a good example of the issues: testing declined from 7,793 per annum to 3,282 in 2020. The UCI also reported a 90 per cent drop in out-of-competition testing. The journalist Andy Brown summarized the situation, although his broad assertion about the impact of testing is questionable. He argued: 'testing has a huge deterrent effect. From March 2020 onwards, this deterrent effect has weakened. Sport's usual defence against athlete doping is down.'[5] Regardless of whether testing does make some athletes think twice about doping, we can say that a lack of testing might embolden athletes whose only reason not to dope is a fear of being caught.

The apparent ineffectiveness of testing has consequences for how we assess the rationale, value and impact of anti-doping. One logical response is that it might not be perfect but the alternatives are worse. Few in sport, government or the wider public interested in sport would be willing to accept giving up all controls and allowing unrestricted doping. There is a powerful consensus around the notion of 'clean sport', and a great deal of anxiety that, if doping was allowed, sport would simply become a free-for-all competition between chemists that could kill athletes. As such, allowing doping is not seen as a possible way forward for sport – even if both these concerns are exaggerated and based on the assumption that all athletes would risk their health and undermine the competitive nature of sport if they had the opportunity to do so.

Yet athletes pay a high price for the pursuit of the mirage or fantasy of 'clean sport', and it would be a mistake to assume that all would dope given an opportunity. The debate has to move beyond simplistic assertions about 'cheating', 'integrity' and 'health', and shift towards recognizing the flaws in the current system. It is only by understanding anti-doping from the athletes' perspective that progress can be made towards a more pragmatic and humane approach. First, we consider how anti-doping can punish the wrong athletes in excessive ways.

Collateral Damage

We define collateral damage as any time an athlete receives a ban that is not for deliberate doping or receives a grossly exaggerated ban that is disproportionate to the circumstances of the doping violation. These cases are the price of clean sport based on individual responsibility and zero-tolerance. We present here only a small selection of examples, as many of these do not reach the public domain.

As discussed in the previous chapter, it is possible for anti-doping laboratories to make mistakes. The experience of Diane Modahl showed that a positive test is extremely hard to disprove or dispute, even if the athlete does have financial resources and access to relevant scientific experts. In recent years, the scientific experts Erik Boye, Jon Nissen-Meyer, Tore Skotland and Bjarne Østerud have reviewed the process of testing for EPO. They have had access to laboratory data for five athletes accused of using EPO who insisted they did not do so. The process of assessing guilt or innocence is complex and subject to interpretation, as it is based on a subjective review of graphs. The Norwegian group have testified in support of two of the athletes, though they have not successfully helped overturn any sanction. The group despaired at the response received from the anti-doping analysts:

> Our argument, as expressed in our expert statement in the hearing for [Norwegian boxer] Hadi Srour, is that any decision requires a quantitative, objective measure of the level of gel staining in the region, i.e. how much EPO-like material is present in the band representing normal, physiological EPO and how much in the region above (rEPO)? To leave this decision to an arbitrary visual inspection of the gels is unscientific. Results from the Norwegian antidoping laboratory and from our own analyses clearly demonstrate that there is no more material in the rEPO-region in the athlete's urine than in a control sample without rEPO, a negative control.[6]

One of the athletes this group tried to help was the Irish runner Steven Colvert. He was banned for two years for EPO use but continued to proclaim his innocence. His sample was destroyed by the laboratory so there was no way to have it retested. The only evidence is the analytical reports, which do not show a high level of EPO measurements. Like other athletes sanctioned for doping, his career has never recovered. He has expressed further concern about the longer-term stigma and impact on his personal and professional life:

> I know I'm forever tarnished with it, especially in the modern age with the Internet and stuff like that. It's something you'll never get away from. If I ever approach an

employer, all they need to do is a quick search and there it is, and there's the back and forth. It's hugely damaging. I understand where people come from when they're skeptical. It's human nature and I just have to accept that.[7]

There are many other athletes who claim that the science of anti-doping has let them down. The English sprinter Callum Priestley was banned for two years after testing positive for clenbuterol. He claimed to have no knowledge of how this might have entered his system, except for possibly through meat he had eaten while on a training visit to South Africa. This sanction ended his career in sport.[8] Another athlete banned for two years for clenbuterol use in 2010 was one of the top professional cyclists in the world, Alberto Contador from Spain. He was stripped of two major wins: the 2010 Tour de France and the 2011 Giro d'Italia. Yet, the amount in his sample was so small that most laboratories did not have equipment sensitive enough to detect clenbuterol at that level. This highlights another issue of anti-doping testing: there are many drugs that are tested for 'presence' rather than a threshold level. This means that regardless of whether a minuscule amount is very unlikely to make any difference to their performance, if it is present in a sample at any level, it is a violation. Like Priestley and other athletes, Contador claimed it came from food:

It is a tremendous injustice . . . I don't give importance to what might appear on paper; it is about my own feeling. It's something I'm going to have for my whole life. But it will not change anything and the people that have shown interest know that it is one of the biggest injustices that has happened in sport.[9]

Even more basic situations can badly affect athletes. The Mexican fencer Paola Pliego missed the 2016 Olympics after different results were returned for her two samples. Her A sample was first analysed after the Pan American Fencing Championships in Panama in June and showed a trace amount (540 nanograms) of modafinil. The B sample was tested in a different laboratory and returned a negative result. She was therefore cleared of any wrong-doing and not banned. But the consequence of this mistake was a hugely significant omission from the Olympics.[10] Missing the Olympics for a sport like fencing can have devastating effects on an athlete's career.

The concern that an athlete might be trying to beat the testers by using masking agents has also led to many unfair decisions. In 2003 Shane Warne, regarded as one of the world's greatest cricketers, was sent home from the World Cup for using a weight-loss supplement that was banned because it could potentially mask steroid use. He was also banned for twelve months despite explaining that his mother had unknowingly given him the tablets.[11] The context does not suggest he intended to cheat by taking steroids as those would increase his muscle strength and distort the very skill he was legendary for – spin bowling.

In 2006 the American skeleton racer Zach Lund thought that he was fine to continue using finasteride for baldness, as he had done for seven years previously. He did not check the 2005 update to the 'List of Prohibited Substances and Methods', which included finasteride, and went on to test positive. He was removed from the 2006 Olympics and stripped of his second-place finish in the World Cup. Finasteride was then removed from the banned list in 2007. It had been placed on the list as a potential masking agent for steroid use, but WADA scientists concluded that it did not have this effect.[12] In other words, Lund missed the high point of his career due to a mix of excessive suspicion, changes in the list he overlooked and inconsistently applied scientific knowledge.

The most famous case of an athlete using a medical drug over a long period of time without realizing it had been put on the

'List of Prohibited Substances and Methods' is that of tennis star Maria Sharapova. She was banned for using meldonium, which was added to the list on 1 January 2016. She claimed not to have learned of this change and continued to use it for health reasons, as she had done for over ten years. Her initial two-year ban was reduced to fifteen months, but the whole episode impacted her career and income from sponsors.

Athletes not being available for testing can also be the cause of excessive sanctions and inconsistencies. The English athlete Christine Ohuruogu was banned for one year for missing three tests in 2006. By contrast, Mark Dry, a Scottish hammer thrower, was given a four-year ban because he missed one test, panicked and lied about where he actually was at the time. The impact on him was clear from his statement:

> This is absolutely game over for me. Financially, it's destroyed me and my family to try and defend myself, which we can't really afford to do. But I will not sit down on this and be bullied because I'm poor. I know I'm not a big-name athlete and that's fine, it's not why I'm in this. But it shouldn't be about how much money you have, or who you're connected to. It should be about what's right and what's wrong and this is not right. This is a huge miscarriage of justice and it's just dangerous and disappointing and really disheartening.[13]

In response, the chief executive of UK Anti-Doping, Nicole Sapstead, defended the decision by saying that Dry had committed a 'serious breach' of the rules that 'undermines the anti-doping process which athletes and the public depend on to have confidence in clean sport'.[14] Dry might feel aggrieved when his case is compared to leading cyclist Lizzie Armitstead (now Lizzie Deignan), who missed three doping tests, which should have led to a two-year ban. In what was no doubt an expensive process involving highly paid lawyers, Armitstead appealed through CAS, which ruled in her favour on the basis of the circumstances leading to the missed tests, with one of them being deemed accidental, one blamed on support staff not completing the forms properly and one on family reasons leading to changing plans at short notice. Yet Nicole Sapstead was somewhat more supportive, saying she agreed with CAS (while awaiting the full explanation), and as a general point said: 'I'd like to think that we are a reasonable organisation and we don't bring cases against athletes unless we see reason for doing so.'[15] It is unclear how or why Dry's case was treated differently, apart from Dry's inability to appeal.

A more tragic outcome occurred when Jarrod Bannister died of suicide. We cannot know the full reasons for his decision; however, he had been banned from sport for twenty months after missing anti-doping tests. For one of them, the DCO was told by reception staff at a hotel that he had checked out. Instead, he was in the hotel and sharing a room with a teammate, but the room was booked by Athletics Australia, so Bannister's name was not on the booking.[16] Another athlete who died by suicide after receiving a ban for doping was the English rugby league player Terry Newton. Others have discussed their struggles with depression, including Danish cyclist Michael Rasmussen. While the cause and effect are debatable, it is likely that a doping ban contributed to their personal and emotional struggles.

The mistaken use of a banned medicine has been at the centre of many disproportionate cases. A substance taken to help cure an ailment, help with sleep or relieve pain can lead to a ban from sport, despite the lack of performance-enhancing benefits. The Norwegian skier Therese Johaug used a lip balm to treat a severe sore on the advice of her team doctor, but the balm contained a banned steroid. She was sanctioned with a ban from sport for eighteen months, which meant she missed the 2018 Winter Olympics. This is a controversial case because the packaging of the

Therese Johaug, banned from sport for using a lip balm.

lip balm contained a clear warning about doping, but the doctor claimed not to have noticed. The amount of the drug in Johaug's system suggested nothing untoward occurred. However, the length of the ban seems harsh given the athlete's intention simply to treat a sore on her lip.

Another set of inadvertent breaches relate to contamination. There are many instances in which the athlete used a nutritional supplement, but the production process led to the supplement becoming contaminated with a banned substance. Appeals in such cases are rarely successful due to the difficulties in identifying the source of the contamination and that the burden of proof is on the athlete to demonstrate the circumstances were not intentional. Even then, the athlete is only likely to get a reduction, not a full exoneration. A handful of cases of human-contact contamination have been successfully appealed. The Canadian Paralympian Jeff Adams proved the cocaine found in his sample came from a woman he met on a night out. However, his case took two years to resolve and effectively ended his career. Again, the expense, time and publicity surrounding such cases can deter many athletes from making an appeal. Their only other choice is to accept the sanction and be banned. The range of contamination circumstances have included food, drinks and even a local water supply. The draconian nature of the strict liability principle can lead to many unfair outcomes.[17]

Amateur Athletes

Elite athletes often have support staff, so even if they make occasional mistakes they have someone looking out for them (though even then mistakes can be made). Elite athletes are also afforded anti-doping educational workshops and are made aware that doping will potentially cost them their career. The situation is very different for athletes who compete at lower levels or have come into competitive sport later in life. Even if they know the broad rules of anti-doping, it is very possible that no one would have told them about the intricacies of policies and substances, or the inadvertent traps awaiting them.

A Welsh rugby player, Shaun Cleary, was banned after cocaine was found in his urine sample taken after a rearranged friendly fixture. He had used the drug several days before but it was still in his system. He was banned for two years, despite never having received anti-doping education or advice, or playing at a competitive level where testing was not a regular occurrence.

The Dutch runner Hinke Schokker started racing in her thirties. At age 35, she tested positive for a substance she had used for decades to treat ADHD, modafinil. Use of modafinil is allowed out of competition but not in competition, due to the stimulating nature of the drug. She took it four days before a race and the sample she provided at the time of the event was found to contain a low amount. The process of making a decision on Schokker's fate took over a year (partially delayed due to the COVID-19 pandemic), and she was eventually banned for eighteen months. By this stage, she had retired from the sport out of disillusionment and the need to focus on her non-sport career. Schokker was critical of 'the actions of the Athletics Union. According to her, the sports association has failed to make it clear to her that her drug use would be in violation of the doping regulations. Because if that had happened, she could have applied for dispensation for the use of her ADHD drug and used it without any problems.'[18]

Another example of injustice relates to a handful of cases in the USA, where older male athletes were prescribed testosterone by their doctors to address health issues. In two such cases the athletes Jeff Hammond and Roger Wenzl were in their sixties and had not received any anti-doping education. Hammond chose to stop training and competing in cycling while using a hormone treatment. Wenzl asked for advice but instead was target tested, returned a positive test, was banned for two years and tragically died of cancer while the label of doper was unfairly applied to him.[19]

These cases of amateur athletes demonstrate the reach of WADA's authority. Anyone who is a member of a club that is itself part of a sports federation that is a signatory to the WADC is under the authority of WADA and its stakeholders. They can be tested any time, on any day, and they can be banned from sport for violations they do not understand. Once banned, these athletes face the 'prohibited association' rule, which means they cannot attend training or competition events. In the worst-case scenarios, they cannot take their own children to local sports classes and tournaments. The reach of anti-doping is extensive and many amateur athletes are unaware of how they could be affected. The ideals of 'clean sport' come at a heavy price.

Memorial to Tommy Simpson on Mont Ventoux.

Engaging Athletes and Addressing Organized Doping

Anti-doping is based on the suspicion that any athlete might dope if they had the opportunity. It is based on stereotypes, perpetuated by surveys purporting to show that athletes would risk their lives for sporting success, including through doping, and on the notion that considerable numbers of athletes are intentionally cheating. Titles of books dramatize this, such as Barrie Houlihan's 2002 analysis, published by the Council of Europe, titled *Dying to Win: Doping in Sport and the Development of Anti-Doping Policy*. The front cover of Houlihan's book is a grainy black-and-white photograph of Tommy

Simpson, looking exhausted, shortly before his collapse on Mont Ventoux. Even those researchers undertaking prevalence surveys may fail to stop and reflect that an athlete admitting to doping at any time over the past twelve months might not have used prohibited substances in a deliberate sense or on a regular basis. Indeed, they might even have successfully requested a therapeuticuse exemption. Much as the media has at times presented doping as a 'moral panic', some academics have helped to perpetuate the idea that doping is commonplace and that athletes would take potentially fatal risks if there were no anti-doping policy to stop them.

However, the evidence is contradictory. One way researchers have tried to assess and predict doping is through social psychological instruments, including the Performance Enhancement Attitude Scale (PEAS). These studies do not support the assumption that athletes would dope if they had the opportunity. For example, a 2018 study using the PEAS for a sample of 340 Polish athletes found that attitudes favourable towards doping were higher among powerlifters and weightlifters, but overall the results showed athletes are in favour of anti-doping.[20] Such studies also cannot link attitudes or views with actual behaviour. Just because an athlete thinks doping may be acceptable in some ways, this in itself does not mean that athlete has or ever will engage in doping.

There are policy implications of the simplistic stereotyping of athletes. One key issue is that current athletes who would be subject to its prohibitions were not consulted on the WADC. This demonstrates a lack of trust that athletes could collectively have a responsible say in how they are regulated. Yet one of the main problems with the one-size-fits-all approach is that not all types of doping are relevant for all sports. Athletes could easily be consulted on the pertinent types of substances and methods for their particular discipline. Engaging athletes in a conversation about what sport means could lead to broader acceptance of the logic of performance enhancement and finding better ways to manage athletes' need for improvement and progress. This is especially important as sporting careers are notoriously perilous. Some research has shown that athletes are at higher risk of doping during 'moments of temptation', or rather, moments of desperation. These might include when facing injury, potential deselection from a team, or trying to move to the next level in sport. In these moments, it might be a nutritional supplement or a medicine they turn to, not necessarily powerful doping drugs. Understanding and empathizing might be more humane, and might lead to better policies, than the immediate assumption that some form of cheating will occur.

Research also shows that athletes are generally supportive of the principles of anti-doping but are concerned about the practicalities. In a 2016 study of 261 elite athletes from 51 different countries and four international sports federations, Anna Efverström and colleagues found that 'athletes did not question the legitimacy of the rules, but had concerns about the legitimacy of the way the rules and principles are enforced in practice, specifically with regard to matters of privacy, lack of efficiency and equal conditions as well as athletes' involvement in the anti-doping work.'[21] Marie Overbye's research has shown that while most Danish athletes surveyed were satisfied with the operations of their own country's anti-doping system, they questioned others: 'A majority of the athletes who had an opinion on the subject regarded testing programmes in some countries as not extensive enough or believed that in certain countries doping control was downgraded to win medals.'[22]

This was reinforced by research undertaken by John Gleaves and Ask Vest Christiansen. They also found that athletes 'generally express contentment with the current system and its ambitious aim to homogenise anti-doping efforts'. However, the more specific details were contentious:

athletes have also raised serious concerns on four specific issues, namely on a), the fair and consistent application of the rules for all athletes in a sport, b) the obligation to submit their whereabouts, c) the due processes when facing accusations of violations and d) the possibility for athletes to genuinely participate in the policy and decision making process.[23]

Such findings reflect the increasingly vocal criticism of WADA coming from athletes such as the Canadian Beckie Scott and UK athletes Callum Skinner and Ali Jawad. More specifically, the recent accusation levelled at WADA is that it did not do enough to sanction Russia for its systematic doping programme. Athletes feel betrayed when obvious, organized cheating is not punished.

A Way Forward

It is worth remembering that the framework for anti-doping was set in the 1960s and focused on stimulants and medal winners. The simple idea was that if two athletes were similarly matched, one should not be allowed to win by benefiting from the short-term boost provided by artificial stimulants. Over time, this framework was extended as health fears meant that all athletes would be governed by anti-doping regulations. The connection was severed between doping and utility: it did not matter if the doped athlete achieved a better outcome. What mattered was upholding the rules and imposing punishments.

As it became harder to ensure that everyone was following the rules, the disempowerment of athletes – based on unfounded suspicions and the belief that all athletes were willing to die for their medals – meant that strict liability and excessive surveillance were forced on them. Any complaint could easily be rebuffed as undermining the aim of clean sport. Any relativizing of the issue based on other forms on inequality – economic, social, political – could be refuted as ignoring the health risks of doping and the integrity of sport. Even scientific research became less concerned with the need for regulation and more focused on the nature of the rules, how to understand athletes' potential risk factors and how to support prevention strategies.

Our question is whether it is possible to design a system of doping control that might predict and prevent organized doping while at the same time avoiding unnecessary punishments of individual athletes. Anti-doping has to become better at stopping another Russia situation, or smaller groups collectively deciding to dope, or corrupt leaders forcing, allowing and covering up doping. However, it also needs to improve the situation of athletes who do not want to be monitored all day every day or risk inadvertent violations ruining their sporting careers and severely damaging their personal and professional lives.

A first broad proposal is to change how 'doping' is understood by the public, by explaining what enhancement means through a more open discussion of the nature of sport. Performance-enhancing methods are essential to success in sport. Athletes are, to use John Hoberman's concept, 'mortal engines', the focus of scientific analysis at every stage of their career progression. Equipment, training strategies, psychological interventions, diet, rest and sleep and their overall lifestyle are all part of the logic and methods of performance enhancement. The 'List of Prohibited Substances and Methods' is not a mechanism for 'pure' sport in the sense proposed by amateur idealists in the mid-twentieth century. There is no drug-free sport anymore and certainly no sport that is not enhanced in one way or another. The list is merely an arbitrary line in the sand rather than an attempt to define the difference between 'acceptable' and 'unacceptable' substances or methods on the basis of existing science and contemporary ethics. Moreover, many of the substances are listed before any research has been conducted on their actual potential to pose health risks or their value in terms of performance enhancement. The list is speculative and based on the subjective judgement of a small group of scientists who remain anonymous.

A shift in understanding would then allow action to be taken on our second proposal: change the criteria on which decisions to prohibit a substance or method are based. As we have noted, the current policy is based on two out of three criteria, which refer to health, performance enhancement and the 'spirit of sport'. We suggest instead that policy be based on a two out of two format. The superfluous and vague 'spirit of sport' criterion would be removed. Therefore, for any substance or method to be banned it must be both a risk to athletes' health and have a demonstrated performance-enhancing effect. Ideally, both criteria must be evidence-based and not speculative. Further, we would suggest that certain substances only be prohibited past established threshold levels, the point of consumption where health is at risk and performance is enhanced. Trace amounts of substances would fit neither criteria. Moreover, recreational drugs would not fit the criteria and would be left to national and local governments to regulate. These changes would be more efficient by making it cheaper to run tests and reducing the number of appeals based on innocuous or inadvertent circumstances. Further, sports federations could select the substances and methods to be prioritized for control in their sport. Most importantly, it would prevent athletes from being sanctioned for inadvertent or recreational use of substances.

Our third proposal is about protecting athletes, focusing on three elements of education, testing and sanctions. With regard to the first of these, there should be a requirement that athletes receive education about these issues in a holistic sense. They should learn what performance enhancement means in an ethical sense, what is risky for their physical and emotional well-being, what exactly is banned, how to avoid inadvertent doping and the preferred nutritional approaches to performance enhancement depending on their sport, age and level of competition. Importantly, they should not be drug tested until they have received this education. In practice, this might mean they cannot compete at a national level until they are educated or that testing may not be done at amateur and recreational levels. Younger athletes need even more protection and their parents should be part of their educational process.

A testing system should remain in place, but it should be more reasonable. Athletes should be allowed time off, including holidays and evenings/nights at home. Drug control officers should not have to come into their homes; alternative methods should be considered, such as having localized testing centres where feasible. The observation of sample delivery should be sensible and humane. WADA should find methods for which direct observation is not required. Sceptics would argue that cheating athletes would find ways to swap urine samples if they were not closely watched. However, there are many stories about unnecessary observation, and it is both obvious and urgent that for younger athletes in particular a stranger should not follow them to the toilet and insist they expose their genitalia.

These critical issues are caused by the reliance on urine samples to detect doping substances. Therefore, a solution for the global sports authorities to consider is to focus more on methods of analysis that do not require a urine sample. In 2010 a group of scientists led by Nawed Deshmukh developed a hair analysis test for two of the commonly used steroids, nandrolone and stanozolol (though we cannot assume that all athletes have sufficient hair to test). They identified steroid use in eleven out of 180 participants' samples. There are some potential risks from this method regarding the timing and level of consumption in relation to competition. Nonetheless, it is worth noting the authors' implied critique of urine testing and identification of the need for change:

> The results obtained demonstrate the application of these hair analysis methods to detect both steroids at low

concentrations, hence reducing the amount of hair required significantly. The new methods complement urinalysis or blood testing and facilitate improved doping testing regimes. Hair analysis benefits from non-invasiveness, negligible risk of infection and facile sample storage and collection, whilst reducing risks of tampering and cross contamination. Owing to the wide detection window, this approach may also offer an alternative approach for out-of-competition testing.[24]

Sanctions need to remain in place but should be targeted at the worst offenders and enablers. Athletes who test positive should be allowed a rapid outcome appeals opportunity, ideally before any publicity about their violation. If they can provide strong evidence that the positive test was inadvertent, the sanction should be reduced. If there is no clear benefit in terms of competition results and based on the amount in the sample, the violation and sanction should be annulled. Where guilt is established, the athletes' support personnel should be investigated and potentially sanctioned. If there is evidence of coercion, the punishments should be increased appropriately for the offender and reduced for the athlete. Punishments should be based on context: the amount of prior anti-doping education they had received, the level of health risk, the extent of performance enhancement and the competitive situation for which doping might have made a difference. If sanctions are publicly announced, details should be provided that relate to the specific violation. Under the current system, all doping cases look the same as the announcement usually simply states that the athlete has tested positive and has received a sanction. However, not all sanctions emerge from deliberate cheating and that should be conveyed in any formal communication.

Our fourth proposal emphasizes the need for an equitable system across all countries that addresses support for education, testing and the costs of making appeals. A centralized financial model should monitor spending per athlete in each country and support those countries that are not able to contribute at the same level as their wealthier peers. Moreover, there should be an independent agency to review the activities of sports organizations, especially where any suspicions have been raised about potential corruption, cover-ups or disengagement from anti-doping. There should also be a system of auditing the fairness, consistency and proportionality of sanctions, with clarity and widespread availability of legal aid funding for athletes who cannot pay for their own legal counsel. A longstanding concern is that testing varies widely across countries. The gaps in testing need to be addressed. This could be done by having sport federations follow a benchmarking system of the number of tests to be conducted, following guidelines of focusing on elite athletes. Testing science is only useful for improving fairness if applied evenly across the global athletic community.

Crucially, these changes should be made in discussion with WADA and athlete representative groups. The future of anti-doping should be realistic rather than idealistic, athlete-centric rather than top-down, educational and supportive rather than punitive, and focused on the areas of highest risk.

If athletes are to be included in governance and decision-making, some recognition should be made of the efforts of existing athlete representative groups to raise key issues. The World Players Association represents athletes from over one hundred athlete associations covering more than sixty sports. In a policy brief document, it summarized its priorities:

> Many player associations are concerned that the World Anti-Doping Agency ('WADA') Code (coupled with the governing structures and roles of WADA and the International Council for the Arbitration of Sport ('ICAS')) have delivered a global anti-doping regime that is:

1. ineffective in protecting sport from doping and, therefore, safeguarding the interests of clean athletes; and
2. unfair and disproportionate, with substantial penalties being imposed on athletes who are not 'cheats'.

Their broad solution is that anti-doping policy should not be decided by one organization with global authority, but – as some professional u.s. team sports already do – should involve athlete collective bargaining. The aim would be to develop rules that are appropriate for each sport, are effective and fair, and are agreed to by the athletes they affect. The World Players Association also proposed more detailed issues to be resolved:

Recognition of the athlete representatives chosen by the players themselves;
Sound and independent governance of anti-doping policy and enforcement;
Reliable and transparent science;
A focus on catching cheats, and not 'inadvertent dopers' and other technical rule breaches;
Acknowledgement of the fundamental human rights of athletes;
Tough yet proportionate penalties;
Adaptation for the needs of professional team sports;
Fair and independent arbitration system;
Substances of addiction and abuse dealt with through rehabilitation;
Effectiveness of anti-doping policy to be objectively and transparently measured and assessed.

To travel such a road is to come a long way from the draconian ambitions that WADA set out in the first WADC and that it has sought to extend ever since. It would involve starting to trust athletes rather than viewing them all as potential dopers, and beginning to respect their basic human rights and civil liberties. It is time to see sport as their job, not their entire lifestyle, and to realize that a forced break from their job – or even forced retirement – is a dramatic loss of income, social networks, reputation and identity that can destroy them. If anti-doping is truly about protecting athletes' health by any measure, WADA needs to rethink its approach.

However, it is essential that athletes are consulted in an organized way that respects their views. The current consultation process for the WADC revisions includes all stakeholders, meaning that athletes' comments can be subsumed within the broader range of submissions. We suggest that a new consultation is introduced that is exclusively for athletes, including recreational, sub-elite and youth athletes. The consultation could take the form of a global survey, translated into multiple languages and conducted on an annual basis. The answers would be anonymized so athletes feel able to be honest. The survey would be disseminated and the results collected by an independent organization, and then summarized in a report presented to WADA and all major sports federations and event organizers. WADA would need to accept the recommendations, or at least provide very good justifications for not doing so. The focus of the survey could be on how athletes perceive the strengths and weaknesses of the current system, as well as what they would like to change and why. Results can be differentiated by type of sport (individual versus team), country, gender, age and level of competition, to look for any patterns. Changes can then be implemented accordingly.

Overall, the proposals we have made here will only be worthwhile if they support athletes. Collecting evidence of what athletes would like to change would provide a much stronger basis for making any policy proposals. The answers are not easy and will take time. However, there are some signs that WADA may listen.

For example, the 2021 WADC includes a reduction in bans for recreational drug use to a standard three months. While we are critical of aspects of the WADC, we are not completely pessimistic about future developments. New initiatives need to be openly discussed, and athletes should be front and centre of the process. Only then will the failures and the critical issues of anti-doping be properly addressed. The history of anti-doping demonstrates that traditional authoritarian models have harsh outcomes and limited success. The future of anti-doping can be different – more democratic, humane and respectful – but only if athletes are engaged with and listened to.

References

1 The Origins of Doping and Anti-Doping in Modern Sport

1 W. Vamplew, *Pay Up and Play the Game* (Cambridge, 1988); R. Holt, *Sport and the British: A Modern History* (Oxford, 1990).
2 J. A. Mangan, ed., *Pleasure, Profit, Proselytism: British Culture and Sport at Home and Abroad, 1700–1914* (London, 1988).
3 W. Vamplew, 'Playing with the Rules: Influences on the Development of Regulation in Sport', *International Journal of the History of Sport*, XXIV/7 (2007), pp. 843–71.
4 P. Dimeo, *A History of Drug Use in Sport, 1876–1976: Beyond Good and Evil* (London and New York, 2007).
5 R. Christison, 'Observations on the Effects of Cuca, or Coca, the Leaves of Erythroxylon Coca', *British Medical Journal*, I (1876), pp. 527–31.
6 D. Courtwright, *Forces of Habit: Drugs and the Making of the Modern World* (Cambridge, MA, and London, 2001), p. 48.
7 G. Andrews and D. Solomon, 'Coca and Cocaine: Uses and Abuses', in *The Coca Leaf and Cocaine Papers*, ed. G. Andrews and D. Solomon (New York and London, 1975).
8 J. S. Haller Jr, 'The History of Strychnine in the Nineteenth-Century Materia Medica', *Transactions and Studies of the College of Physicians of Philadelphia*, XL (1973), pp. 226–38; p. 236.
9 T. A. Cook, *The Fourth Olympiad, London Official Report* (London, 1908).
10 Dimeo, *A History of Drug Use in Sport*.
11 R. Beamish and I. Ritchie, 'From Fixed Capacities to Performance-Enhancement: The Paradigm Shift in the Science of "Training" and the Use of Performance-Enhancing Substances', *Sport in History*, XXV (2005), pp. 412–33.
12 J. Hoberman, *Mortal Engines: The Science of Performance and the Dehumanization of Sport* (New York, 1992).

13 L. Knighton, *Behind the Scenes in Big Football* (London, 1948), p. 74.

14 Ibid., pp. 74–7.

15 Dimeo, *A History of Drug Use in Sport*, p. 45.

16 P. Karpovich, 'Ergogenic Aids in Work and Sport', *Research Quarterly for the American Physical Education Association*, XII (1941), pp. 432–50; p. 432.

17 J. Gleaves and M. Llewellyn, 'Sport, Drugs and Amateurism: Tracing the Real Cultural Origins of Anti-Doping Rules in International Sport', *International Journal of the History of Sport*, XXXI/8 (2014), pp. 839–53.

18 Ibid., pp. 842–3.

19 International Amateur Athletic Federation, Annual Meeting Minutes, 1928, Section 17, Report by Mr Genet of France, 'appearance money', IOC Archives, p. 55, cited in Gleaves and Llewellyn, 'Sport, Drugs and Amateurism', p. 846.

20 O. Reisser, 'Über Doping and Dopingmittel, *Leibseübungen und körperliche Erziehung*', pp. 393–4, cited in Hoberman, *Mortal Engines*, p. 131.

21 A. Brundage, handwritten note (undated, likely 1937), Box 77, Folder 'IOC Meeting Minutes', Brundage Archives, cited in Gleaves and Llewellyn, 'Sport, Drugs and Amateurism', p. 849.

22 Bulletin officiel du Comité International Olympique, 1938, p. 30. Lausanne: International Olympic Committee. Accessed through the LA84 Foundation website: www.la84.org, cited in I. Ritchie, 'Pierre de Coubertin, Doped "Amateurs" and the "Spirit of Sport": The Role of Mythology in Olympic Anti-Doping Policies', *International Journal of the History of Sport*, XXXI/8 (2014), pp. 820–38; p. 828.

2 Speed and Steroids

1 N. Rasmussen, *On Speed: The Many Lives of Amphetamines* (New York, 2008), p. 54.

2 Ibid., p. 71.

3 C. Woodward, *New York Times*, 1 October 1948.

4 M. Novich, 'Use and Misuse of Drugs to Improve Athletic Performance', in *Proceedings of the International Congress of Sport Sciences,* ed. K. Kato (Tokyo, 1964).

5 A. Gold, 'International Policy and Philosophy of Drug Control in Sport', in *Drug Abuse in Sport: Report of a Sports Council Symposium for Governing Bodies*, 27 March 1985 (London, 1986).

6 Rasmussen, *On Speed*, p. 193.

7 Ibid., p. 85.

8 *The Times*, 6 June 1957.

9 *New York Times*, 7 June 1957.

10 *New York Times*, 8 June 1957.

11 *New York Times*, 8 June 1957.

12 R. H. Raynes, 'The Doping of Athletes', *British Journal of Sports Medicine*, 4 (1969), pp. 145–62; p. 148.

13 G. Pirie, *Running Wild* (London, 1961), pp. 28–9.

14 Cited in W. Fotheringham, *Put Me Back on My Bike: In Search of Tom Simpson* (London, 2007), p. 160.

15 Council of Europe, *Council of Europe Committee for Out-of-School Education, Doping of Athletes: Reports of the Special Working Parties* (Strasbourg, 1964).

16 *Daily Mail*, 10 September 1962.

17 *Sunday People*, 13 September 1964.

18 *The Times*, 12 September 1964.

19 B. Weiss and V. G. Laties, 'Enhancement of Human Performance by Caffeine and the Amphetamines', *Pharmacological Reviews*, xiv/1 (1962), pp. 1–36; p. 6.

20 Ibid., pp. 1–36; p. 32.

21 P. Dimeo, *A History of Drug Use in Sport, 1876–1976: Beyond Good and Evil* (London and New York, 2007), p. 44.

22 P. Karpovich, 'Ergogenic Aids in Work and Sport', *Research Quarterly for the American Physical Education Association*, xii (1941), pp. 432–50.

23 P. De Kruif, *The Male Hormone* (New York, 1947) cited in W. Taylor, *Macho Medicine: A History of the Anabolic Steroid Epidemic* (London, 1991), p. 16.

24 E. Simonsen, W. C. Kearns and N. Enzer, 'Effect of Methyl Testosterone Treatment on Muscular Performance and the Central Nervous System of Older Men', *Journal of Clinical Endocrinology*, iv/11 (1944), pp. 528–34.

25 Cited in J. Hoberman, *Testosterone Dreams: Rejuvention, Aphrodisia, Doping* (Berkeley, ca, 2005), p. 3.

26 J. Fair, 'Isometrics or Steroids? Exploring New Frontiers of Strength in the Early 1960s', *Journal of Sport History*, xx/1 (1993), pp. 1–24.

27 Ibid.

28 Ibid., p. 23.

29 T. McNab, 'Why Do Competitors Take Drugs?', in *The 4th Permanent World Conference on Anti-Doping in Sport, 5–8 September 1993, Conference Proceedings* (London, 1993).

30 A. H. Payne, 'Anabolic Steroids in Athletics (Or the Rise of the Mediocrity)', *British Journal of Sports Medicine*, IX/2 (1975), pp. 83–8.

31 B. Gilbert, 'Drugs in Sport: Problems in a Turned-On World', *Sports Illustrated*, 23 June 1969, pp. 64–72.

32 Payne, 'Anabolic Steroids in Athletics', p. 83.

33 T. M. Hunt, *Drug Games: The International Olympic Committee and the Politics of Doping, 1960–2008* (Austin, TX, 2011).

34 N. Rose, 'Neurochemical Selves', *Society*, XLI (2003), pp. 46–59.

3 The Beginnings of Testing

1 T. M. Hunt, *Drug Games: The International Olympic Committee and the Politics of Doping, 1960–2008* (Austin, TX, 2011), p. x.

2 O. Schantz, 'The Presidency of Avery Brundage, 1952–1972', in *The International Olympic Committee – One Hundred Years, Part II*, ed. R. Gafner (Lausanne, 1994).

3 P. Dimeo, *A History of Drug Use in Sport, 1876–1976: Beyond Good and Evil* (London and New York, 2007), p. 90.

4 A. Venerando, 'Italian Experiments on the Pathology of Doping and Ways to Control It', in Council of Europe, *Council of Europe Committee for Out-of-School Education, Doping of Athletes: Reports of the Special Working Parties* (Strasbourg, 1964), p. 49.

5 Ibid., p. 50.

6 Ibid., p. 48.

7 Council of Europe, 'Doping in Sport', Committee on Culture and Education, 18 April 2000.

8 Council of Europe, *Council of Europe Committee for Out-of-School Education, Doping of Athletes*, p. 4.

9 Ibid., pp. 4–5.

10 L. Prokop, 'The Problem of Doping', in *Proceedings of International Congress of Sport Sciences*, ed. K. Kato (Tokyo, 1964), p. 269.

11 Council of Europe, *Council of Europe Committee for Out-of-School Education, Doping of Athletes*, p. 6.

12 Venerando, 'Italian Experiments on the Pathology of Doping', p. 53.

13 *Bulletin du Comité Internationale Olympique* (February 1962), p. 46.

14 G. La Cava, 'The Use of Drugs in Competitive Sport', *Bulletin du Comité Internationale Olympique* (1962), p. 53.

15 K. Henne, 'The Emergence of Moral Technopreneurialism in Sport: Techniques in Anti-Doping Regulation, 1966–1976', *International Journal of the History of Sport*, XXXI/8 (2014), pp. 884–901.

16 J. Santos and M. Pini, 'Doping', *Bulletin du Comité Internationale Olympique* (1963), p. 57.

17 A. Porritt, 'Doping', *Journal of Sports Medicine and Physical Fitness*, v (1965), p. 166.

18 J.G.P. Williams, 'Doping of Athletes', *Physical Education*, LV (1963), p. 40.

19 Prokop, 'The Problem of Doping', p. 286.

20 IOC, 63rd IOC Session Minutes, 6–10 October 1964, p. 10.

21 L. Woodland, *Dope: The Use of Drugs in Sport* (London, 1980), pp. 108–9.

22 L. Prokop, 'Drug Abuse in International Athletics', *Journal of Sports Medicine*, III/2 (1975), p. 86.

23 S. Green, 'Tour of Britain: 1965 Doping Scandal Remembered', BBC, www.news.bbc.co.uk, 14 September 2012.

24 A. Beckett, 'Philosophy and Practice of Control of Drug Abuse in Sport, Part 1', in *Development of Drugs and Modern Medicines: A Conference to Honour Professor Arnold H. Beckett*, ed. J. W. Gorrod, G. G. Gibson and M. Mitchard (Chichester, 1986), p. 566.

25 Cited in R. Beamish and I. Ritchie, 'From Chivalrous "Brothers-in-Arms" to the Eligible Athlete: Changed Principles and the IOC's Banned Substance List', *International Review for the Sociology of Sport*, XXXIX/4 (2004), pp. 355–71; p. 361.

26 IOC, 65th IOC Session Minutes, 6–9 May 1967.

27 Swedish Olympic Committee, 'Hans-Gunnar Liljenvall, Modern Pentathlon', https://sok.se/idrottare/idrottare/h/hans-gunnar-liljenvall.html, accessed 4 October 2021.

28 Cited in W. Fotheringham, *Put Me Back on My Bike: In Search of Tom Simpson* (London, 2007), p. 148.

29 Ibid., p. 166.

4 How Doping Became an Epidemic

1 P. Dimeo, *A History of Drug Use in Sport, 1876–1976: Beyond Good and Evil* (London and New York, 2007), p. 116.

2 P. Dimeo, T. M. Hunt and R. Horbury, 'The Individual and the State: A Social Historical Analysis of the East German "Doping System"', *Sport in History*, XXXI/2 (2011), pp. 218–37.

3 *The Guardian*, 23 August 1972.

4 Quoted in *The Times*, 14 October 1972.

5 Cited in *Timeshift: Drugs in Sport*, BBC, www.bbc.co.uk/news, 15 June 2005.

6 L. Woodland, *Dope: The Use of Drugs in Sport* (London, 1980), p. 57.

7 Quoted in *The Times*, 24 August 1972.
8 T. M. Hunt, P. Dimeo, F. Hemme and A. Mueller, 'The Health Risks of Doping during the Cold War: A Comparative Analysis of the Two Sides of the Iron Curtain', *International Journal of the History of Sport*, XXXI/17 (2014), pp. 2230–44.
9 K. Patera, cited in T. Todd, 'Anabolic Steroids: The Gremlins of Sport', *Journal of Sport History*, XIV/1 (1987), pp. 87–107; p. 95.
10 Ibid.
11 C. Dubin, *Commission of Inquiry Into the Use of Banned Practices Intended to Increase Athletic Performance* (hereafter Dubin Report) (Ottawa, 1990), pp. 228–9.
12 Ibid., p. 239.
13 Cited in F. Landry and M. Yerlès, *The International Olympic Committee: One Hundred Years. The Idea, the Presidents, the Achievements* (Lausanne, 1996), p. 255.
14 M. Killanin, *My Olympic Years* (London, 1983), p. 161.
15 R. S. Laura and S. W. White, 'The Price Athletes Pay in Pursuit of Olympic Gold', in *Drug Controversy in Sport: The Socio-Ethical and Medical Issue*, ed. R. S. Laura and S. W. White (Sydney, 1991), p. 6.
16 *The Times*, 21 April 1972.
17 N. A. Sumner, 'Measurement of Anabolic Steroids by Radioimmunoassay', *Journal of Steroid Biochemistry*, V (1974), p. 307; R. V. Brooks, R. G. Firth and D. A. Sumner, 'Detection of Anabolic Steroids by Radioimmunoassay', *British Journal of Sports Medicine*, IX/2 (1975), pp. 89–92; A. Beckett, 'Problems of Anabolic Steroids in Sport', *Olympic Review*, CIX–CX (1976), pp. 591–8.
18 A. Kicman and D. B. Gower, 'Anabolic Steroids in Sport: Biochemical, Clinical and Analytical Perspectives', *Annals of Clinical Biochemistry*, XL (2003), pp. 321–56.
19 Ibid.
20 J. Krieger, *Dope Hunters: The Influence of Scientists on the Global Fight Against Doping in Sport, 1967–1992* (Champaign, IL, 2016).
21 'Blagoy Blagoev', www.sportsreference.com, accessed 6 September 2021.
22 Beckett, 'Problems of Anabolic Steroids in Sport', p. 597.
23 T. M. Hunt, P. Dimeo, M. T. Bowers and S. R. Jedlicka, 'The Diplomatic Context of Doping in the Former German Democratic Republic: A Revisionist Examination', *International Journal of the History of Sport*, XXIX/18 (2012), pp. 2486–99.
24 Final Report of the President's Commission on Olympic Sports (Washington, DC, 1977), vol. I, p. 123.

25 Dubin Report, pp. 229–30.
26 Dubin Report, p. 240.
27 Final Report of the President's Commission on Olympic Sports (1977), vol. I, pp. 251–2.
28 T. Hunt, *Drug Games: The International Olympic Committee and the Politics of Doping, 1960–2008* (Austin, TX, 2011), p. 66.
29 R. Ruiz, 'The Soviet Doping Plan: Document Reveals Illicit Approach to '84 Olympics', *New York Times*, 13 August 2016.
30 Krieger, *Dope Hunters*, p. 202.
31 J. Krieger, L. P. Pieper and I. Ritchie, 'Sex, Drugs and Science: The IOC's and IAAF's Attempts to Control Fairness in Sport', *Sport in Society*, XXII/9 (2019), pp. 1555–73.
32 I. Ritchie and G. Jackson, 'Politics And "Shock": Reactionary Anti-Doping Policy Objectives in Canadian and International Sport', *International Journal of Sport Policy and Politics*, VI/2 (2014), pp. 195–6; p. 195.
33 Ibid., pp. 195–6.
34 Ibid., p. 196.
35 'Weightlifter Still Stigmatized 20 Years After Pan Am Scandal', CBC, 7 February 2002, at www.cbc.ca.
36 Ibid.
37 Ritchie and Jackson, 'Politics And "Shock"'.
38 A. J. Ryan. 'Anabolic Steroids Are Fool's Gold', *Federation Proceedings*, XL/12 (1981), pp. 2682–8; p. 2682.
39 S. Assael, *Steroid Nation: Juiced Home Run Totals, Anti-Aging Miracles, and a Hercules in Every High School: The Secret History of America's True Drug Addiction* (New York, 2007), p. 5.
40 Ibid.
41 Dubin Report, pp. 229–30.

5 The End of Innocence

1 D. Wharton, 'Olympic La-La Land', *Los Angeles Times*, 4 August 2009.
2 S. Assael, *Steroid Nation: Juiced Home Run Totals, Anti-Aging Miracles, and a Hercules in Every High School: The Secret History of America's True Drug Addiction* (New York, 2007), p. 26.
3 T. M. Hunt, *Drug Games: The International Olympic Committee and the Politics of Doping, 1960–2008* (Austin, TX, 2011), pp. 75–6.
4 Ibid., p. 76.
5 I. Waddington, 'Doping in Sport: Some Issues for Medical Practitioners', Play the Game Conference, 12 November 2002.

6 A. Shipley, 'Sprinter Issajenko Unrepentant About Using Drugs',
   Washington Post, 22 September 1999.
7 B. Beacon, 'Four Members of Canada's National Weightlifting Team
   Have Been . . .', www.upi.com, 4 November 1983.
8 'From Gold and Silver to Drugs and Jail: David Jenkins Never Ran
   from Fate', *The Scotsman*, 9 July 2012; M. Macaskill, 'McMaster Calls
   for Doping Inquiry', *The Times*, 24 April 2016.
9 *The Times*, 16 December 1987, cited in I. Waddington, 'Changing
   Patterns of Drug Use in British Sport from the 1960s', *Sport in
   History*, xxv/3 (2005), pp. 472–96; p. 478.
10 T. Sanderson, *Tessa: My Life in Athletics* (London, 1986), p. 159.
11 Cited in P. Coni, G. Kelland and D. Davies, *Amateur Athletics
   Association Drug Abuse Enquiry Report* (London, 1988), paragraph B25.
12 Waddington, 'Changing Patterns of Drug Use in British Sport from
   the 1960s', p. 492.
13 G. A. Condit, Memorandum to Assembly Subcommittee on Sports
   and Entertainment of California Legislature, 4 December 1985,
   Todd-McLean Collection, University of Texas at Austin, p. 2.
14 C. Dubin, *Commission of Inquiry Into the Use of Banned Practices
   Intended to Increase Athletic Performance* (hereafter Dubin Report)
   (Ottawa, 1990), p. 365.
15 W. E. Buckley et al., 'Estimated Prevalence of Anabolic Steroid Use
   among Male High School Seniors', *Journal of the American Medical
   Association*, CCLX/23 (1988), pp. 3441–5.
16 T. Symonds, untitled study (attached to 'Assemblyman Introduces
   Steroid Legislation', News from Assemblyman Gary Condit,
   4 December 1985), p. 5, Todd-McLean Collection, University of Texas
   at Austin.
17 U.S. House of Representatives, Hearing Before the Subcommittee
   on Crime of the Committee on the Judiciary on H.R. 4658: Anabolic
   Steroids Control Act of 1990 (Washington, DC, 1990).
18 'Drinking Too Much Coffee Could Disqualify Olympians', *Lakeland
   Ledger*, 8 February 1982.
19 J. Gleaves, 'Manufactured Dope: How the 1984 U.S. Olympic Cycling
   Team Rewrote the Rules on Drugs in Sports', *International Journal
   of the History of Sport*, XXXII/1 (2015), pp. 89–107; p. 102.
20 Dubin Report, p. 285.
21 Ibid., p. 298.
22 Ibid., p. 308.
23 Ibid., p. 340.
24 Ibid., p. 336.

25 A. Kuriloff, 'Steroids Put Bulge in Pockets', ESPN, 15 March 2005.

26 S. Harrah, 'Dan Duchaine Unchained', www.musclenet.com, accessed
    6 September 2021.

27 Dubin Report, p. 345.

28 J. Cart, 'World Anti-Doping Conference Was a Challenge Itself',
    Los Angeles Times, 18 July 1988.

29 'Johnson Home in Disgrace; Canada Bans Him for Life: Can't Run
    for Country or Get Funds', *Los Angeles Times*, 27 September 1988.

30 Council of Europe, Anti-Doping Convention (Strasbourg),
    16 November 1989.

31 Ibid.

32 Dubin Report, p. 541.

33 R. Harvey, 'Defectors Expose E. German Doping: Two Former
    Sports Officials Describe Methodical Administration of Drugs',
    Los Angeles Times, 15 July 1989.

34 M. Fisher, 'East German Doping Detailed in Documents: Steroids:
    Widespread Program Included Seven Olympic Gold Medalists. Drug
    Efficiency Tested on Children in Sports Camps', *Washington Post*,
    7 September 1991.

35 W. Franke and B. Berendonk, 'Hormonal Doping and Androgeniza-
    tion of Athletes: A Secret Program of the German Democratic
    Republic Government', *Clinical Chemistry*, XLIII/7 (1997), pp. 1262–79.

36 J. Hoberman, *Mortal Engines: The Science of Performance and the
    Dehumanization of Sport* (New York, 1992), pp. 1–2.

6 Facing Up to the Scandals

 1 T. M. Hunt, P. Dimeo, F. Hemme and A. Mueller, 'The Health Risks
    of Doping During the Cold War: A Comparative Analysis of the
    Two Sides of the Iron Curtain', *International Journal of the History
    of Sport*, XXXI/17 (2014), pp. 2230–44.

 2 R. Terney and L. McLain, 'The Use of Anabolic Steroids in High
    School Students', *American Journal of Diseases in Children*, CXLIV/1
    (1990), pp. 99–103.

 3 Ibid., p. 99.

 4 C. Yesalis, N. Kennedy, A. Kopstein and M. Bahrke, 'Anabolic-
    Androgenic Steroid Use in the United States', *Journal of the American
    Medical Association*, CCLXX/10 (1993), pp. 1217–21.

 5 H. M. Perry, D. Wright and B.N.C. Littlepage, 'Dying to Be Big:
    A Review of Anabolic Steroid Use', *British Journal of Sports Medicine*,
    XXVI/4 (1992), pp. 259–61.

6 D. Williamson, 'Anabolic Steroid Use Among Students at a British College of Technology', *British Journal of Sports Medicine*, XXVII/3 (1993), pp. 200–201.

7 Ibid., p. 200.

8 P. Korkia and G. Stimson, 'Indications of Prevalence, Practice and Effects of Anabolic Steroid Use in Great Britain', *International Journal of Sports Medicine*, XVIII/7 (1997), pp. 557–62.

9 M. Janofsky, 'Barcelona; Female U.S. Shot-Putter Banned After Drug Test', *New York Times*, 9 August 1992.

10 M. Janofsky, 'Barcelona; Banned American Explains Use of Drug', *New York Times*, 7 August 1992.

11 '"Disgraced" Davies Is Olympic Coach', *Daily Mail*, 19 August 2008.

12 BBC, 'Krabbe Receives IAAF Settlement', www.bbc.co.uk/news, 30 April 2002.

13 H. McIlvanney, 'End of the World for Diego Maradona', *The Times*, 3 July 1994.

14 D. Modahl, *The Diane Modahl Story: Going the Distance. The Heartbreaking Truth Behind the Headlines* (London, 1995), p. 190.

15 M. Rowbottom, 'Athletics: Slaney Doping Ban Upheld at IAAF Hearing', *The Independent*, 26 April 1999.

16 D. Baron, D. Martin and S. A. Magd, 'Doping in Sports and Its Spread to At-Risk Populations: An International Review', *World Psychiatry*, VI/2 (2007), pp. 118–23.

17 J. Brant, 'Playing Dirty', *Outside* (July 1999), www.outside.com.

18 M. Rendell and S. Horsdal, 'Life after Lance', *The Observer*, 2 July 2006.

19 Baron et al., 'Doping in Sports and Its Spread to At-Risk Populations', p. 121.

20 Ibid., p. 122.

21 B. López, 'The Invention of a "Drug of Mass Destruction": Deconstructing the EPO Myth', *Sport in History*, XXXI/1 (2011), pp. 84–109; p. 89.

22 L. Fisher, 'Stamina-Building Drug Linked to Athletes' Deaths', *New York Times*, 19 May 1991.

23 M. Bamberger, 'Over the Edge Aware that Drug Testing Is a Sham, Athletes Seem to Rely More Than Ever on Performance Enhancers', *Sports Illustrated*, 14 April 1997.

24 Ibid.

25 J. Lichfield, 'Allez le Tour', *The Independent*, 2 July 1999.

26 'The Drugs Scandal Update', www.cyclingnews.com, 26 July 1998.

27 IOC, Lausanne Declaration on Doping in Sport, 4 February 1999.

28 R. Coomber, 'How Social Fear of Drugs in the Non-Sporting World Creates a Framework for Doping Policy in the Sporting World', *International Journal of Sport Policy and Politics*, VI/2 (2014), pp. 171–93.

7 A New Approach

1 IOC, 'Major Advances in the Fight Against Doping Meant that the Olympic Games Sydney 2000 Represented a Landmark Moment for the Olympic Movement, in Several Ways', www.olympic.org, 20 November 2020.

2 'The 2000 Olympics: Games of the Drugs?', *CBSNews*, 31 January 2002.

3 Ibid.

4 V. Chaudhary, 'Bitter Pill as Tiny Gymnast Loses Gold', *The Guardian*, 29 September 2000.

5 T. Humphries, 'Drug User's Power of Positive Thinking', *Irish Times*, 10 July 2000.

6 J. Christie, 'Six Austrians Banned from Olympics in Turin Doping Scandal', *Globe and Mail*, 25 April 2007.

7 'Ferdinand Banned for Eight Months', *The Guardian*, 19 December 2003.

8 World Anti-Doping Agency, 'Fundamental Rationale for the World Anti-Doping Code', *World Anti-Doping Code* (Montreal, 2021), p. 13.

9 K. Grohmann, 'Sprinters' Doping Saga Still Haunts Greece', *Reuters*, 8 July 2008.

10 'Bush Calls for Anti-Doping Effort', CNN, 21 January 2004.

11 V. Conte, cited in BBC, 'Conte's Prescription for Success', www.bbc.co.uk/news, 16 May 2008.

12 J. Calvert, G. Arbuthnott and B. Pancevski, 'Revealed: Sport's Dirtiest Secret', *The Times*, 2 August 2015.

13 R. Ulrich et al., 'Doping in Two Elite Athletics Competitions Assessed by Randomized-Response Surveys', *Sports Medicine*, XLVIII/1 (2018), pp. 211–19.

14 D. Mackay, 'Record Number of London 2012 Disqualifications Shows Justice Been Served, WADA President Claims', www.insidethegames.biz, 13 August 2020.

15 T. Fordyce, 'Lance Armstrong: Fall of a Sporting Hero', www.bbc.co.uk/news, 11 October 2012.

16 L. Clarke, 'Spanish Cycling Speaks Out over Saiz', *Cycling News*, 24 May 2006.

17 BBC, 'Operation Puerto: Spanish Legal System "Thwarted" Anti-Doping Investigation', www.bbc.co.uk/news, 26 September 2019.

18 'UCI Announces Anti-Doping Measures in Response to CIRC', www.velonews.com, accessed 6 September 2021.

19 L. Ostlere, 'McLaren Report: More Than 1,000 Russian Athletes Involved in Doping Conspiracy', *The Guardian*, 9 December 2016.

20 A. Ybarra, 'Beckie Scott, WADA Athletes Committee Calls for Full Russian Ban', *Associated Press*, 8 December 2019.

8 Problems and Proposals

1 I. Waddington and V. Møller, 'WADA at Twenty: Old Problems and Old Thinking?', *International Journal of Sport Policy and Politics*, XI/2 (2019), pp. 219–31.

2 A. Brown, 'Romanian NADO Instructed Lab to Cover Up Positive Tests', www.sportsintegrityinitiative.com, 14 June 2019.

3 S. Ingle, 'How Lamine Diack's 16-Year Reign in Charge of IAAF Led to a Jail Term', *The Guardian*, 17 September 2020.

4 O. de Hon, H. Kuipers and M. van Bottenburg, 'Prevalence of Doping Use in Elite Sports: A Review of Numbers and Methods', *Sports Medicine*, XL/1 (2015), pp. 57–69.

5 A. Brown, 'Decline in Testing in Tennis Illustrates Impact of Covid-19 on Anti-Doping', www.sportsintegrityinitiative.com, 4 February 2021.

6 E. Boye, 'Detection of Recombinant EPO and Innocent Athletes', Perspectives on Doping and Anti-Doping series, International Network for Doping Research, 1 December 2020.

7 'I Have Never Doped So to Be There at All Was Shocking to Me', www.the42.ie, 14 October 2016.

8 A. Kessel, 'Callum Priestley Suspended After Positive Drugs Test', *The Guardian*, 5 March 2010.

9 H. Robertshaw, '"One of the Biggest Injustices in Sport": Alberto Contador Still Angry At Doping Ban and Loss of Grand Tour Titles', *Cycling Weekly*, 26 September 2017, www.cyclingweekly.com.

10 N. Butler, 'Mexican Fencer Cleared of Wrongdoing After Re-Analysis of "Positive" Drug Test', www.insidethegames.biz, 18 October 2016.

11 C. De Silva, 'Shane Warne Recalls Biggest Regret from 2003 Suspension for Banned Substance', wwos.nine.com.au, 12 May 2020.

12 'Zach Lund Takes Break from Skeleton', www.espn.com, 12 November 2010.

13 D. Roan, 'Mark Dry: Hammer Thrower Says Doping Ban Is Miscarriage of Justice', BBC, www.bbc.co.uk/news, 14 May 2020.

14 Ibid.

15 'Rio 2016 Olympics: Lizzie Armitstead Defends Missed Drugs Tests', BBC, www.bbc.co.uk/news, 3 August 2016.

16 J. Austin, 'Jarrod Bannister Dead: Commonwealth Games Gold Medallist Dies Suddenly Aged 33', *The Independent*, 9 February 2018.

17 P. Dimeo and V. Møller, *The Anti-Doping Crisis in Sport: Causes, Consequences, Solutions* (London and New York, 2018).

18 S. Anderson, 'Hinke Schokker, Suspended Due to Doping, Has Let Go of Athletics', *Leeuwarder Courant*, 24 June 2020, http://lc.nl; see also H. Schokker, Perspectives on Doping and Anti-Doping series, International Network for Doping Research, 15 March 2021.

19 Dimeo and Møller, *The Anti-Doping Crisis in Sport*.

20 K. Sas-Nowosielski and A. Budzisz, 'Attitudes Toward Doping among Polish Athletes Measured with the Polish Version of Petroczi's Performance Enhancement Attitude Scale', *Polish Journal of Sport and Tourism*, XXV/2 (2018), pp. 10–13.

21 A. Efverström, N. Ahmadi, D. Hoff and Å. Bäckström, 'Anti-Doping and Legitimacy: An International Survey of Elite Athletes' Perceptions', *International Journal of Sport Policy and Politics*, 8 (2016), pp. 491–514; p. 491.

22 M. Overbye, 'Doping Control in Sport: An Investigation of How Elite Athletes Perceive and Trust the Functioning of the Doping Testing System in Their Sport', *Sport Management Review*, XIX/1 (2016), pp. 6–22; p. 6.

23 J. Gleaves and A. V. Christiansen, 'Athletes' Perspectives on WADA and the Code: A Review and Analysis', *International Journal of Sport Policy and Politics*, XI/2 (2019), pp. 341–53; p. 341.

24 N. Deshmukh et al., 'Analysis of Anabolic Steroids in Human Hair Using LC-MS/MS', *Steroids*, LXXV/10 (2010), pp. 710–14; p. 710.

Further Reading

Andreasson, J., and A. Henning, *Performance Cultures and Doped
    Bodies: Challenging Categories, Gender Norms, and Policy Responses*
    (Champaign, IL, 2021)
Assael, S., *Steroid Nation: Juiced Home Run Totals, Anti-Aging Miracles,
    and a Hercules in Every High School: The Secret History of America's
    True Drug Addiction* (New York, 2007)
Beamish, R., and I. Ritchie, *Fastest, Highest, Strongest: A Critique of
    High-Performance Sport* (London and New York, 2006)
Chambers, D., *Race Against Me: My Story* (London, 2009)
Dasgupta, L., *The World Anti-Doping Code: Fit for Purpose?* (Oxford, 2019)
—, *Doping in Non-Olympic Sports: Challenging the Legitimacy of WADA?*
    (Oxford, 2022)
Dimeo, P., *A History of Drug Use in Sport, 1876–1976: Beyond Good
    and Evil* (London and New York, 2007)
—, and Møller, V., *The Anti-Doping Crisis in Sport: Causes, Consequences,
    Solutions* (London and New York, 2018)
Dubin, C., *Commission of Inquiry Into the Use of Banned Practices Intended
    to Increase Athletic Performance* (Ottawa, 1990)
Fainaru-Wada, M., and L. Williams, *Game of Shadows: Barry Bonds,
    Balco, and the Steroids Scandal that Rocked Professional Sports*
    (New York, 2006)
Fincouer, B., J. Gleaves and F. Ohl, eds, *Doping in Cycling:
    Interdisciplinary Perspectives* (London and New York, 2020)
Gleaves, J., and T. M. Hunt, *A Global History of Doping in Sport: Drugs,
    Policy, and Politics* (London and New York, 2015)
Hamilton, T., and D. Coyle, *The Secret Race: Inside the Hidden World
    of the Tour de France: Doping, Cover-ups, and Winning at All Costs*
    (London, 2012)

Henne, K., *Testing for Athlete Citizenship: Regulating Doping and Sex in Sport* (New Brunswick, NJ, 2015)

Hoberman, J., *Mortal Engines: The Science of Performance and the Dehumanization of Sport* (New York, 1992)

—, *Testosterone Dreams: Rejuvenation, Aphrodisia, Doping* (Berkeley, CA, 2005)

Houlihan, B., *Dying to Win: Doping in Sport and the Development of Anti-Doping Policy* (Strasbourg, 2002)

Hunt, T. M., *Drug Games: The International Olympic Committee and the Politics of Doping, 1960–2008* (Austin, TX, 2011)

Krieger J., *Dope Hunters: The Influence of Scientists on the Global Fight Against Doping in Sport, 1967–1992* (Champaign, IL, 2016)

McArdle, D., *Dispute Resolution in Sport: Athletes, Law and Arbitration* (London and New York, 2015)

Mazanov, J., *Managing Drugs in Sport* (London and New York, 2018)

Millar, D., *Racing Through the Dark: The Fall and Rise of David Millar* (New York, 2011)

Modahl, D., *The Diane Modahl Story: Going the Distance. The Heartbreaking Truth Behind the Headlines* (London, 1995)

Møller, V., *The Ethics of Doping and Anti-Doping: Redeeming the Soul of Sport?* (London, 2010)

—, I. Waddington, and J. Hoberman, eds, *Routledge Handbook of Drugs in Sport* (London, 2017)

Read, D., J. Skinner, D. Lock and A.C.T. Smith, *WADA, the World Anti-Doping Agency: A Multi-Level Legitimacy Analysis* (London and New York, 2021)

Rodchenkov, G., *The Rodchenkov Affair: How I Brought Down Russia's Secret Doping Empire* (London, 2020)

Taylor, W., *Macho Medicine: A History of the Anabolic Steroid Epidemic* (London, 1991)

Waddington, I., and A. Smith, *An Introduction to Drugs in Sport: Addicted to Winning?* (London and New York, 2009)

Walsh, D., *Seven Deadly Sins: My Pursuit of Lance Armstrong* (London, 2012)

—, *The Russian Affair: The True Story of the Couple Who Uncovered the Greatest Sporting Scandal* (London, 2021)

Woodland, L., *Dope: The Use of Drugs in Sport* (London, 1980)

Acknowledgements

We have several people to thank for their support during the writing of this book. We'd like to thank, first, David Watkins and Martha Jay at Reaktion Books, who guided us through the editing process. We also have several individuals in our field to thank. Jesper Andreasson's feedback and suggestions throughout were invaluable. Jörg Krieger, Verner Møller, Ask Vest Christiansen and John Gleaves offered insights and general support for our work. We also owe a debt of gratitude to the members of the International Network of Doping Researchers (INDR) who have informed our work over the past several years. Our friends and colleagues at the University of Stirling were also key to keeping us going on this project. David McArdle was central to the idea for this book and keeping us on track. We'd also like to thank Stephen Morrow and Colin Moran for their continuous support. Finally, we also thank our s3rg colleagues. Cheers!

Photo Acknowledgements

The author and publishers wish to express their thanks to the below sources of illustrative material and/or permission to reproduce it. Every effort has been made to contact copyright holders; should there be any we have been unable to reach or to whom inaccurate acknowledgements have been made, please contact the publishers, and full adjustments will be made to subsequent printings.

Collection Jules Beau, Gallica Digital Library: p. 17; Peter Curbishley: p. 202; Dutch National Archives: pp. 25, 74, 85, 91; Fotocollectie Anefo: pp. 95, 97; International Olympic Committee: p. 21; Los Angeles Times Photographs Collection: p. 58; National Library of Medicine: p. 20; Reuters/ Alamy Stock Photo: p. 147; Stadtarchiv Kiel: p. 83; Wellcome Trust: p. 18; Wikimedia Commons: pp. 24, 66, 96, 161, 168, 180, 181, 182, 199.

Index

Page numbers in *italics* indicate illustrations